To the people who welcomed me back home with open arms

Anne Faber is a TV chef and food journalist based in Luxembourg.

Born and raised in Luxembourg, Anne moved to the UK in 2003 to pursue her studies. She graduated with an MA in English Literature from University College London (UCL) and went on to do a postgraduate degree in Journalism at City University London, specializing in food and drink writing.

Anne has worked as a TV producer for APTN, ZDF and RTL, and ate her way around London as a restaurant critic for Time Out London. In 2010, she started her food blog Anne's Kitchen, which was awarded a Digital Food Award by Food & Wine magazine in the US in 2013.
Anne accomplished a culinary training course at Alain Ducasse in Paris in 2015.

Anne's first cookbook, which was published in 2013, focused on British cuisine. Her second cookbook (2014) featured recipes inspired by her travels to Barcelona, Istanbul and Berlin. Both books were awarded the Luxembourg Book Prize. In this third cookbook, Anne explores the cuisine of her homeland, Luxembourg. Anne has her own prime time TV show on RTL Télé Letzebuerg, which accompanies her books.

www.anneskitchen.co.uk

EDITIONS SCHORTGEN

Recipes & Food Photography
ANNE FABER

Photography Véronique Kolber

ANNE'S
KITCHEN®

This book started out as a way to reconnect with Luxembourg, my homeland. After 12 years of living in the UK I decided that it was time for a change. So I packed up my life and moved back to the country I had left over a decade ago.

Arriving back in Luxembourg was interesting. Flash-backs of my life as a teenager mixed with constant wonder of how much had changed in this small country. People kept on asking me whether I missed London and commented on how quiet it must be in contrast here. The strange thing is: I wasn't missing a thing. I felt right at home.

I suddenly remembered the excitement of the first white asparagus arriving on market stalls, the pure delight of picking rhubarb from the garden, the *Quetschefester* and innumerable village fêtes celebrating seasonal produce. London might have been exciting, but it could at times feel slightly disconnected from actual reality.

As I started adapting to the Luxembourg pace of life, my cooking changed too. I found myself turning towards more local and seasonal ingredients and looking out for the classic flavours of my childhood to integrate in my cooking.

However, me being me, I didn't feel like purely recreating classic Luxembourg dishes. In London I had gotten used to eating fusion cuisine on a daily basis, and I wasn't going to change that variety in Luxembourg...

So instead, I took to adding unconventional flavours to traditional staples and integrate Luxembourg ingredients in international dishes. I threw our beloved *Judd mat Gaardebounen* into a blender and made a cannelloni stuffing with it, I bestowed our sacred *Rieslingspaschtéit* with an Indian touch and I turned *Träipen* an all their trimmings into one scrumptious quiche. Yes, you will find some rather exotic ingredients in here, but you can easily get hold of them in most supermarkets.

This book is a reflection of what I eat here and now, in my home, sweet home, Luxembourg. I hope that through my recipes, you will be able to rediscover Luxembourg cuisine and excite your taste buds with new, yet familiar flavours.

E Gudden!

Anne

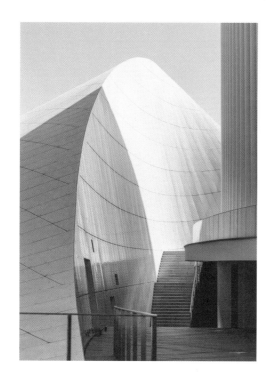
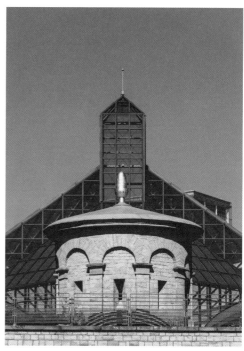

Savoury muffins are the perfect picnic treat, and the best thing is that you can throw anything you have lingering in the fridge into them. For this recipe I have used a Luxembourg cheese called *Berdorfer Roude Bouf*, a lovely hard cheese with a mature taste. I have also added *Mettwurscht*, a very popular smoked sausage that you are bound to find on the barbeque at any Luxembourg village fête.

METTWURSCHT MUFFINS

❀ Makes 54 mini muffins or 9 normal sized muffins • Prep 30' • Oven 12-20' • Easy ❀

3 eggs
50ml olive oil
100ml milk
180g flour
2 tsp baking powder
150g Berdorfer Roude
  Bouf (or mature
  Cheddar or Gruyère)
1 Mettwurscht sausage
salt and pepper

Preheat the oven to 180°C fan.

In a bowl, mix the eggs with the olive oil and milk.

In a separate bowl, mix the flour and baking powder with a pinch of salt and pepper.

Incorporate the egg mixture into the dry mixture.

Grate the cheese and add to the batter.

Cut the Mettwurscht lengthwise in half, scrape out the meat filling with a spoon and roughly chop. Discard the casing and add the meat to the batter.
Mix to combine.

Grease a muffin tin and distribute the batter between the holes.

Bake the mini muffins for 12 minutes or the normal sized muffins for 20 minutes.

These are best served warm.

TIP

You can use chopped up salami instead of *Mettwurscht* or leave out the meat altogether and use chopped olives, sundried tomatoes or smoked salmon instead.

These mini *Gromperekichelcher* will be the star at your next party! Crispy, bite-sized potato morsels topped with sweet apple compote and smoky bacon - what's not to love?!

GROMPEREKICHELCHER BITES

❦ Makes 48 • 2 x 24 hole mini muffin tin • Prep 25' • Oven 20' • Easy ❦

800g floury potatoes
½ onion
¼ tsp salt
sunflower oil
100g smoked bacon
  lardons
1 small jar of apple
  compote
parsley, to decorate

Preheat the oven to 200°C fan.

Peel the potatoes and the onion and finely grate them. Put into a sieve, season with salt, mix well and squeeze out as much liquid as you can.

Pour some sunflower oil into the holes of two 24 hole mini muffin tins.
Fill each hole with the potato mix, pressing down.

Brush the potato mix with some more sunflower oil and bake in the preheated oven for 20-30 minutes until they are golden at the bottom and easily coming out of the tin.

Meanwhile, fry the bacon lardons in a hot frying pan until browned.
Drain on kitchen paper and set aside.

Fill the apple compote into a piping bag.

Once baked, remove the Gromperekichelcher nuggets from the tin with a spoon and put on a serving plate.

Pipe a dollop of apple compote onto each Gromperekichelchen, top with a few bacon lardons and decorate with a bit of chopped parsley.

TIPS

• If you can't get hold of a mini muffin tin, don't be tempted to use a regular-sized muffin tin – the bites won't get as crispy! Instead, you can pan-fry teaspoon-sized portions of the *Gromperekichelcher* mix in a generous amount of oil and reheat them in a hot oven just before your guests arrive.

• The *Gromperekichelcher* nuggets freeze really well. Just pop the frozen bites in a hot oven until warmed through and crispy.

• For a Japanese-inspired variation, pipe some *okonomiyaki* sauce from page 102 and mayonnaise onto the *Gromperekichelcher*.

I love throwing big parties with lots of food – but usually there's just not enough time to spend days slaving away in the kitchen to produce a whole myriad of bite-sized nibbles. This recipe is perfect for when you have lots of guests coming and you would rather not spend endless time preparing finger food. These swirls taste best straight out of the oven.

DUO OF PUFF PASTRY SWIRLS

❧ Makes 100 • Prep 20' • Cooling 30' • Oven 15' • Easy ❧

1 Träip or black
   pudding
2 x 230g all-butter
   puff pastry
2 tbsp mustard
150g soft goat's cheese
   with garlic

Peel the Träip, cut into pieces and roughly mash with a fork.

Unroll one puff pastry disc and spread with the Träip, all the way to the edges. Brush the entire Träip surface with mustard.

Cut the puff pastry disc crosswise into 4 pieces. Roll each piece up firmly, starting with the corner where the round edge touches a straight edge and rolling it from the outside in, so that you follow the cut line. Lightly pat down the seam of each roll to seal.

Place the 4 Träip rolls onto a plate and freeze for 30 minutes to firm up.

Meanwhile, unroll the second puff pastry disc and spread with the goat's cheese. Cut the puff pastry disc crosswise into 4 pieces and roll up the same way as the Träip rolls. Put into the freezer for 30 minutes.

Preheat the oven to 200°C fan.

Take out the firm Träip rolls and cut into slices ½ cm thick. One end of the roll will be quite hollow, as the round edge will have rolled up slightly awkwardly– you can merge the last two pieces from the end into one nice swirl, by sticking the very last piece into the hollow centre of the penultimate piece.

Place the swirls onto a baking tray lined with baking paper and bake in the preheated oven for 15 minutes. Repeat with the goat's cheese swirls.

Serve the swirls straight from the oven when still warm.

TIP

You can freeze the uncut puff pastry rolls. Simply defrost for a couple of hours in the fridge before baking, making sure they are still firm enough to cut. Proceed with the recipe as above.

A few weeks before I moved back to Luxembourg, I discovered a lovely local market near my former home in North London. I was pretty gutted that I only found out about Alexandra Palace farmers market just as I was about to leave town. Still, it provided me with the inspiration for this recipe.
One of the market stalls was selling beautiful rye bread studded with nuts and dried fruit, and next to those wonderful bread loaves were a few bags of delicious looking artisanal bread chips.
These crispy crackers totally wowed me – what a perfect, moorish companion for cheese!
As I can no longer just pop back to *Ally Pally* these days to get some more, I decided to make my own version with classic Luxembourg ingredients: walnuts, honey and raisins. The twice-baked process in this recipe is similar to the one in biscotti recipes– it may look like a lot of work but it's actually surprisingly easy, you just need a little bit of time.

WALNUT RAISIN CRACKERS

❧ 2 small loaf tins of 12 x 5 cm • Makes about 50 crackers • Prep 1h30' • Cooling 3h • A little effort ❧

140g flour
1 tsp baking powder
½ tsp rosemary leaves
60g walnuts
60g raisins
25g brown sugar
25g honey
1 tsp salt
250ml buttermilk
pepper
butter, for greasing
olive oil, for brushing

Preheat the oven to 180°C fan.

In a bowl, mix the flour and the baking powder.

Chop the rosemary, walnuts and raisins and add to the bowl together with all the remaining ingredients. Mix so that you get an uniform batter.

Butter 2 small rectangular cake moulds (12x5 cm) and fill each with half the batter.

Bake in the preheated oven for 35 minutes.

Turn the cakes out onto a wire rack and leave to cool completely for about 3 hours.

Once the cakes are completely cold, preheat the oven to 150°C fan.

Cut the cakes into very thin slices and put the slices onto a baking tray lined with baking paper. Brush the top of each cracker with olive oil and bake in the preheated oven for 15 minutes.

After 15 minutes, flip the crackers and bake for another 15 minutes or until they are dried out and crispy.

Put the crackers onto a wire rack to cool.

These keep in a tin for 1 week and taste great on their own, with foie gras or with cheese.

TIP

You can experiment with other exciting flavour combinations like almond and dried apricot, fig and walnut or cranberry and pecan nuts.

Pickling eggs may sound like a strange concept, but in the UK you can find jars of pickled eggs in old pubs and fish and chip shops. These quails' eggs are pickled with beetroot, which gives them a beautiful pink colour. I first made these pickled appetizers around Easter, but they can be enjoyed anytime of the year really. Plus, the beetroot pickle that you're left with is a tasty treat, too!

BEET PICKLED QUAILS' EGGS

❊ Makes 40 halves • Prep 45' • Overnight marinating • A little effort ❊

2 uncooked beetroot
250ml cider vinegar
250ml water
100g sugar
1 tsp coarse grain salt
1 bay leaf
1 tsp black
  peppercorns
a pinch of fennel seeds
20 quails' eggs

To serve:
mayonnaise
black fish roe

Peel the beetroot, grate and put into a saucepan with the cider vinegar, water, sugar, salt and bay leaf. Put the black peppercorns and fennel seeds into a teabag and add to the saucepan. Bring to the boil and stir until the sugar has dissolved.

Take off the heat, remove the teabag with the aromatics and the bay leaf. Leave to cool.

Meanwhile, cook the quail's eggs. Put the eggs into a saucepan with cold water, bring to the boil and simmer for 4 minutes. Drain and rinse under cold water.

Peel the quails' eggs by submerging an egg in a bowl with water and delicately removing the shell under water – this will prevent the egg from tearing too easily.

Put the peeled eggs into a sealable jar. Strain the beetroot pickling liquid through a sieve and cover the eggs with the liquid. If you want to keep the beetroot pickle (see serving suggestions below), put the beetroot and remaining pickling liquid into another sealable jar and store both jars in the fridge.

Leave the eggs to marinate overnight. The next day, take the eggs out of the pickling liquid and cut each egg in half.

Put a dollop of mayonnaise onto each egg half and serve with black fish roe.

TIPS

• For a veggie version, replace the fish eggs with baby cress and mix some wasabi into the mayonnaise.
• The eggs keep in the pickling liquid for up to a week – their lovely pink colour will deepen with time.
• The pickled beetroot is great in a salad, on a goat's cheese toast, with fish fingers or on a burger.
• If you can't be bothered to peel all the quail's eggs, you can buy pre-peeled eggs in the supermarket.

People tend to eat a lot of smoked salmon in Luxembourg, but I think it would be a great idea and more sustainable to serve more local fish. Smoked trout is a great alternative and these smoked trout rolls make for a tasty appetizer at a festive drinks party.

SMOKED TROUT CRÊPE ROLLS

※ Makes 24 • Prep 50' • Cooling 6h • Easy ※

For the crêpes:
1 egg
110ml milk
45g flour
30g butter, melted
10g chives
2 tbsp sunflower oil
salt and pepper

For the filling:
125g smoked trout
  fillets
½ shallot
100g crème fraîche
lemon juice, to taste
1 granny smith apple
capers, to serve
salt and pepper

Start by making the crêpes: In a bowl, mix the egg with the milk, flour and melted butter. Finely chop the chives and add to the batter. Season with salt and pepper.

Heat 1 tablespoon of sunflower oil in a 28 cm frying pan, add half the crêpe batter and cook the crêpe for approximately 2 minutes. Flip and cook on the other side for 1 more minute.

Put the crêpe onto a plate and repeat with the remaining batter. Set the crêpes aside to cool while you make the trout filling.

Check the trout fillets for fish bones; remove them if you find any. Cut the trout fillets into chunks and put into a blender.

Peel and chop the shallot and add to the blender together with the crème fraîche, some lemon juice and a pinch of salt and pepper. Blend into a paste and put into a bowl.

Cut the apple in half, grate one half and squeeze out some of the liquid. Wrap the other apple half in cling film and refrigerate.

Add the grated apple to the trout paste, mix and season with salt and pepper and more lemon juice if needed.

Spread half the trout paste over one crêpe. Roll up the crêpe, wrap in cling film and refrigerate for 6 hours. Repeat with the second crêpe.

Before serving, cut the remaining apple into small cubes and drizzle with a bit of lemon juice. Remove the cling film from the crêpes and cut each crêpe into 12 slices.

Decorate each crêpe roll with a few apple cubes and capers and serve.

TIPS

• During wild garlic season, I would use wild garlic instead of chives in the pancakes.
• If you're in a hurry, you can make the trout paste and spread it on a simple slice of toast, sprinkled with apple cubes and capers.

Over 100.000 residents in Luxembourg are of Portuguese origin – that's impressive, considering that Luxembourg only has a population of about 575.000. For me it was essential to create a dish for this book that celebrates both our cultures and culinary heritages. It was pretty obvious to use *bacalhau*, the dried saltfish that features prominently in Portuguese cuisine and pair it with one of Luxembourg's traditional staples: a *Bouchée à la Reine* (a puff pastry vol-au-vent filled with creamy chicken, mushroom and veal sauce). So, here are my *Mini Bacalhau Bouchées*! By desalting the fish overnight, cooking it in milk and serving it in a creamy white wine béchamel, the *bacalhau* loses its pungent fishiness. I have managed to convert quite a few Luxembourgers with these little appetizers, and my Portuguese friends approve of them, too.

MINI BACALHAU BOUCHÉES

❖ Makes 60 • Prep 1h15' • Overnight soaking • Easy ❖

200g dried bacalhau, in chunks
200ml milk
100ml cream
2 spring onions
30g butter
25g flour
60ml white wine
60 mini bouchée cases
50g cheese, grated
chopped parsley, to sprinkle
salt and pepper

Start by soaking the bacalhau the day before: put the dried fish into a large plastic container and fill with cold water. Close with a lid and refrigerate for 12 hours, changing the water twice during that time.

After 12 hours, drain the bacalhau. Heat the milk and the cream in a saucepan until nearly boiling. Turn down the heat and poach the bacalhau pieces in the simmering liquid for 15 minutes until the fish is so soft it starts to fall apart.

Strain the fish through a sieve, catching the poaching liquid in a bowl. Flake the fish with a fork and set aside to cool.

Finely chop the spring onions.

Heat the butter in a saucepan and fry the spring onions for a couple of minutes. Add the flour and fry on a medium heat for a couple of minutes.

Gradually add the poaching liquid, whisking between each addition and leaving it to cook for a minute or so, so it thickens and you get a smooth sauce. Then gradually add the white wine in the same way. Add the flaked fish and season.

Preheat the oven grill to high.

Put the béchamel into a piping bag. Place the bouchée cases on a baking tray and fill each pastry case with béchamel. Top with some grated cheese and place under the oven grill. Grill the bouchées until the cheese has browned and sprinkle with chopped parsley.

Serve warm.

TIP

You can fill the bouchées with cooled bacalhau sauce and sprinkle the cheese on top up to 2 hours ahead. Take them out of the fridge half an hour before your guests arrive and pop them under the grill to melt the cheese and heat them through.

There was a time when apple roses were all over the internet; food bloggers around the world were going crazy for these neat little rolled-up apple parcels. I wasn't too fussed – 'style over substance' was my verdict. Until I joined the guys from *Lët'z Grill* at the Southwest German BBQ championship. It's there that, to my surprise, I found these hardcore barbecue masters making beautiful, pristine-looking courgette roses as a side to their chicken main! And they were just delicious! Salty, crispy and moreish – the perfect accompaniment. I also learnt that baking on a barbecue is totally doable; so yes, it would be possible to grill these on a closed barbecue, too. Anyway, I would like to thank the *Lët'z Grill* Team for the inspiration, and with a recipe like that, there was no way they were not going to win the championship in the end.

COURGETTE ROSES

❧ Makes 12 • Prep 45' • Easy ❧

1 small courgette
230g all-butter
  puff pastry
100g olive tapenade
12 cherry tomatoes
olive oil, to brush
salt and pepper

Preheat the oven to 200°C fan.

Grease a 12-hole muffin tin.

Trim the courgette and cut into thin slices, preferably with a mandolin.

Roll out the puff pastry and cut crosswise into 4 pieces. Cut each piece into 3 long strips.

Lay out a puff pastry strip in front of you and spread with tapenade.

Arrange some courgette slices lengthwise, in a straight line, overlapping slightly, on the top half of the dough strip. Season with salt and pepper. Fold up the bottom part of the dough and roll the dough up loosely to form a rose shape. Place the rose into the greased muffin hole, making sure there is some room inside the rolled up pastry so the puff pastry can expand. Put a cherry tomato in the middle.

Repeat with the remaining strips.

Brush the courgette tops with a bit of olive oil.

Bake the roses in the preheated oven for 25 minutes.

These can be enjoyed hot or cold.

 TIP   You can use pesto instead of tapenade.

Quesadillas are such a fun and speedy snack: you just stuff some cheese between two tortilla wraps and grill it until the cheese has melted. I have made the quesadillas in this recipe with one of my favourite winter comfort foods - raclette - and filled them with all the traditional raclette sides. Simply divine!

RACLETTE QUESADILLAS

❧ Serves 2 • Prep 15' • Quick & Easy ❧

120g Raclette cheese slices
4 mini tortilla wraps
4 pickled gherkins
12 pickled onions
2 slices of smoked ham
pepper

Cut the rind off the raclette cheese and cut each slice into a few small strips.

Lay out two tortilla wraps and top with ⅔ of the cheese.

Slice the pickled gherkins and onions and scatter over the cheese.

Add the ham slices and top with the remaining cheese. Season with pepper and finish each quesadilla with the remaining tortilla wrap.

Heat a frying pan over a medium heat. Once hot, place one quesadilla into the pan and fry for about 2 ½ minutes. Flip over and fry on the other side for another minute until all the cheese has melted.

Repeat with the second quesadilla.

Cut into triangles and serve while still hot.

TIP

There are endless quesadilla variations! Why not try out the following:
• Butternut squash puree, feta and rosemary
• Blue cheese, red onion and mango chutney
• Cheddar, diced red peppers, onions and jalapeños
• Cheddar, sweetcorn, smoked paprika
• Goat's cheese, tinned pear cubes and *sirop de Liège*

Pumpkin fever spreads around Luxembourg every autumn, and lots of different pumpkin and squash varieties can be found at the local markets. Every year, the village of Beringen holds a popular *Kürbisfest*, which features a contest to crown the biggest pumpkin in the country – some of the contestants are so humongous they scare the living hell out of me, as I'm pretty sure I'd get crushed to death if one of them were to roll over me... Still, I love pumpkins, big or small! Like most Luxembourgers, I make pumpkin soup in autumn, and this is my exotic take on a comforting classic.

COCONUT PUMPKIN SOUP WITH CORIANDER PESTO

🌸 Serves 4 • Prep 50' • Easy • Vegetarian 🌸

1 onion
1,2kg butternut squash
2 tbsp olive oil
1 garlic clove
3 tsp ginger, grated
½ tsp dried chilli flakes
½ tsp cinnamon
700ml vegetable stock
400ml coconut milk
salt and pepper

For the pesto:
½ bunch of mint
½ bunch of coriander
30g unsalted cashew nuts
½ garlic clove
40ml olive oil
a pinch of salt

Peel and finely chop the onion.

Peel and deseed the butternut squash and cut into 2cm chunks.

Heat the olive oil in a heavy-bottomed saucepan and fry the onion for 4 minutes until soft.

Peel and crush the garlic. Add the garlic and ginger to the saucepan and fry for another minute.

Add the butternut squash and a dash of vegetable stock and fry for a couple of minutes to sweat the squash a little. Add the chilli flakes and the cinnamon and fry for another minute.

Pour the remaining stock and the coconut milk into the saucepan and bring to the boil. Cover and cook for about 15 minutes until the squash is soft.

Meanwhile, prepare the pesto: Put all the pesto ingredients into a blender and blitz into a chunky pesto. Set aside.

Once the squash is soft, blend the soup with a stick blender until smooth; season with salt and pepper.

Serve each portion with a dollop of pesto.

TIPS

• If you have any leftover pesto, you can store it in the fridge for up to 1 week by putting it into an airtight container and covering the pesto surface with olive oil.
• If you can't get hold of butternut squash, you can use pumpkin instead.

I am partial to giving traditional Luxembourg dishes an international twist. *Bouneschlupp* is a hearty green bean soup that's specked with bacon lardons and served with a dash of cream. In my previous book, I created a German-inspired *Bouneschlupp*, substituting the cream with cream cheese dumplings. I still really like the idea of adding a filling element to *Bouneschlupp*, so for this version I beefed up my soup with some Asian meatballs. I also added beautifully fragrant herbs to the broth. It might be one step too far for this soup still to be considered a *Bouneschlupp*, but beans are beans after all, and you can still 'schlupp' (slurp) it... So, *Bouneschlupp* it is!

THAI BOUNESCHLUPP

❀ Serves 4 • Prep 1h • Easy ❀

For the soup:
1 shallot
1,2l chicken stock
2 lemongrass sticks
30g ginger
1 red chilli
5 kaffir lime leaves
2 potatoes
250g green beans

For the meatballs:
400g minced pork
1 tbsp lemongrass paste
½ tsp ginger, grated
½ tsp salt
1 red chilli
2 tbsp coriander, chopped
1 garlic clove

Peel the shallot and cut into slices.

Put the chicken stock into a large saucepan and bring to the boil. Wash the lemongrass sticks, then bruise with a pestle. Wash the ginger and cut into slices. Slice the chilli lengthwise (and remove the seeds if you prefer a less spicy soup). Add to the stock together with the shallot slices and kaffir lime leaves. Cover and leave to simmer for 20 minutes.

Meanwhile, peel the potatoes and cut into 1 cm cubes. Trim the beans and cut into bite-sized pieces.

To prepare the meatballs, mix the minced pork with the lemongrass paste, ginger and salt. Destem the chilli, slice open lengthwise, remove the seeds and finely chop. Add the chilli to the meat together with the chopped coriander. Peel and crush the garlic and add to the meat, mix and form 24 little walnut-sized meatballs and put on a plate.

Once the stock has been simmering for 20 minutes, remove the aromatics. Add the potatoes and beans, cover and cook for another 10 minutes.

After 10 minutes, add the meatballs to the broth, cover and leave to simmer for another 5 minutes until the meatballs, potatoes and beans are cooked through. Serve immediately.

 TIP

If you don't have any lemongrass paste, just use 1 tablespoon of grated ginger instead.

Often specked with slices of *Mettwurscht* or bacon lardons, Luxembourg *Lënsenzopp* makes for a hearty, filling meal on a cold day. I have to admit that whenever I cook with lentils, it's mostly to make Indian daals, so when it came to reinterpreting Luxembourgish *Lënsenzopp*, I instantly reached for the spice cupboard. I am infusing a classic lentil soup with some of my favourite warming Indian spices and keeping the soup vegetarian. The naan bread is great for mopping up any soup left at the bottom of the bowl, but you could also serve it with some crusty bread instead.

INDIAN-STYLE LËNSENZOPP

Serves 4 • Prep 1h • Easy • Vegetarian

1 onion
2 carrots
1 potato
1 garlic clove
250 green lentils
2 tbsp sunflower oil
2 tsp garam masala
1 tsp ginger, grated
1 tsp cumin seeds
¼ tsp chilli flakes
1,5l vegetable stock

To serve:
Crème fraîche
Fresh coriander

Start by peeling the onion, carrots and potato. Cut into small cubes and put into separate bowls. Peel and crush the garlic clove.

Rinse the lentils in cold water and set aside.

Heat 2 tablespoons of sunflower oil in a heavy-bottomed saucepan, add the onion and fry for 4 minutes until soft. Add the lentils and fry for another minute.

Add the garlic, garam masala, ginger, cumin seeds and chilli flakes and fry for another minute.

Add the carrots and potatoes and fry for another minute, then add the vegetable stock and bring to the boil.

Cover the saucepan with a lid and leave to simmer for 40 minutes.

While the soup is cooking, prepare the naan bread.

Serve each portion of soup with a dollop of crème fraîche, a sprinkle of coriander and a naan bread.

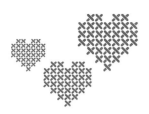

NAAN BREADS

200g flour + extra for dusting
2 tsp baking powder
¼ tsp salt
175g yoghurt
1 tbsp nigella seeds
or 1 tsp cumin seeds
(optional)
olive oil, for frying

Put all the dough ingredients, except the olive oil, into a bowl and mix with a spoon. Once the dough starts to come together, knead briefly with your hands. Leave to rest for 15 minutes.

Cut the dough into 4 parts. Lightly flour the work surface, roll the first piece of dough in the flour, then gently stretch the dough into a disc roughly the size of your hand. You can dip the dough into some more flour if it is too sticky when stretching.

Heat some olive oil in a frying pan and fry the dough discs for 2 to 3 minutes on each side, until the base is cooked and golden brown.

TIPS

• The wetness of the naan dough depends on how liquid the yoghurt is. Add a bit more yoghurt if it feels too dry when you knead it.

• I always keep a batch of these naan breads in the freezer as they are great with any soup, curry or salad.

• If you omit the nigella or cumin seeds, you can even use the dough as a base for a quick 'pizza'. Simply fry the discs on both sides, sprinkle them with cheese and any toppings you like and pop them under the grill for a few minutes until the cheese has melted.

This creamy chicory soup is a firm favourite of mine. It is essential to core the chicory in order to reduce its inherent bitterness. If you still find that your soup tastes too bitter, you can add some more sugar at the end, as that is the secret weapon against bitterness (yes, even in life).

CREAM OF CHICORY SOUP

❦ Serves 4 • Prep 40' • Quick & Easy ❦

3 chicory heads
1 shallot
1 apple
1 potato
20g butter
700ml chicken stock
2 thyme sprigs
50g pancetta or bacon
200ml cream
½ tsp sugar
salt and pepper

Slice the chicory heads lengthwise, trim off the bottoms and cut out the inner, triangular core – this is the bitter part of the chicory. Finely slice and set aside.

Peel and finely chop the shallot. Peel and core the apple. Peel the potato and grate both the apple and potato.

Melt the butter in a saucepan and fry the shallot on a medium heat for about 4 minutes until soft. Add the chopped chicory and sweat for a couple of minutes.

Add the grated apple, potato, chicken stock and thyme sprigs to the chicory. Cover and bring to the boil. Simmer for 10 minutes.

Meanwhile, finely chop the bacon and fry in a dry frying pan until crispy. Drain on kitchen paper and set aside.

After 10 minutes, take the saucepan off the heat. Take out the thyme sprigs, add the cream and sugar and blend into a smooth soup with a hand blender. Season with salt and pepper to taste.

Serve the soup sprinkled with fried bacon.

I'd never eaten, let alone made nettle soup before shooting with Cindy of *De Grénge Schapp* for my show. Cindy took me to the *Mëllerdall* (a region in the East of Luxembourg dubbed 'Little Switzerland'), where we foraged for wild nettles (see the note below) and cooked a nettle soup. I have to say, at first I was a little apprehensive of eating nettles – surely those thick stalks and stingy leaves can't taste very nice? – but I was pleasantly surprised. In this soup, the nettles wilt and become soft and silky, a bit like spinach leaves. Paired with the bold flavour of Luxembourg *Mettwurscht*, this makes for a lovely foraged meal on the wild side.

NETTLE SOUP FROM 'DE GRÉNGE SCHAPP'

❀ Serves 4 • Prep 1h • Easy ❀

1 onion
1 small leek
1 fennel bulb
4 handfuls trimmed
  and washed nettles
  (see tip below)
400g new potatoes
30g butter
2 garlic cloves
1 tbsp summer savoury
  (Bounekräitchen)
1.2l water
4 Mettwurscht
sausages
cream, to serve
salt and pepper

Peel and finely chop the onion. Trim the leek, cut lengthwise, then cut into slices and wash. Trim the fennel bulb and cut into small dice. Roughly chop the nettles and set aside.

Wash the new potatoes and cut the unpeeled potatoes into 2 cm cubes. Set aside.

Melt the butter in a large saucepan and fry the onion with a pinch of salt for 4 minutes until soft. Add the leek and fennel and sweat for a couple of minutes.

Peel and crush the garlic cloves and add to the onions, fry for another minute.

Add the nettles and fry until they have wilted completely.

Add the summer savoury, potatoes, water and a good pinch of salt. Cover and bring to the boil, then simmer for 20 minutes until the potatoes are cooked through.

Meanwhile, cut the Mettwurscht sausages lengthwise in half and fry in a dry frying pan until browned. Cut into bite-sized chunks and set aside.

Add the Mettwurscht pieces to the soup when you're ready to serve, adjust the seasoning with salt and pepper.

Serve each portion of soup with a dash of cream.

TIPS

• You won't find nettles on supermarket shelves, so put on your wellies, grab some gardening gloves, and it's off to the fields or the forest! Generally nettle season starts in April and runs until the end of July. It's best to pick young nettles that don't have seeds growing on them yet, as old nettles tend to be quite woody and not very pleasant to eat. Thoroughly wash the nettles with plenty of water. Once they're wet, the nettles should no longer sting. Remove the stalks and only keep the leaves for cooking.

• If you don't want to go foraging for this recipe you can either use young spinach leaves or sorrel instead. Or make the recipe with French beans, in which case it will turn into a *Bouneschlupp* of sorts.

Nothing beats a hearty onion soup on a cold winter's day! I make mine with Luxembourgish beer and pimp it with little bacon dumplings for extra texture.

ONION SOUP WITH
BEER & BACON DUMPLINGS

❦ Serves 4 • Prep 1h 15' • Easy ❦

7 onions
20g butter
1 tbsp sunflower oil
a few thyme sprigs
2 tbsp sugar
2 tbsp flour
300ml Wëllen
　Ourdaller beer or ale
1.3l vegetable stock
1 bay leaf
2 cloves
2 tbsp Worcestershire
　sauce
1 tbsp Port wine
　(optional)

For the dumplings
(makes about 24):
120g flour
1 tsp baking powder
100g smoked bacon
　lardons
20g butter, melted
salt and pepper

Peel the onions, halve and cut into slices.

Heat the butter and the oil in a heavy-based saucepan and gently fry the onions with the thyme and a pinch of salt over a medium heat for 15 minutes until meltingly soft and browned.

Meanwhile, prepare the dumplings. Put the flour and baking powder into a bowl.

Finely chop the bacon lardons and fry in a pan until cooked through.
Add to the flour together with the melted butter, season with salt and pepper.
Add 4 tablespoons of water and mix with a spoon until the dough comes together, then knead into an elastic dough with your hands.

Form 24 hazelnut-sized balls out of the dough and place onto a plate.

After 15 minutes, remove the thyme sprigs from the onions, add the sugar and fry for 2 minutes, then add the flour and fry for another minute.

Add the beer, vegetable stock, bay leaf, cloves and Worcestershire sauce to the onions.

Bring to the boil, add the dumplings and reduce the heat to a simmer.

Cover the saucepan and cook for 15 minutes, then uncover and cook for another 15 minutes.

Before serving, add the Port wine and adjust the seasoning with salt and some more Worcestershire sauce, if needed.

TIP

You can sprinkle some grated cheese over the soup before serving. Alternatively, a friend suggested serving this soup with a '*Moschterschmier*' – a slice of toasted bread smothered in Luxembourg mustard. And yes, it really is a brilliant fit!

At the beginning of spring you can find wild garlic growing in the forests in and around Luxembourg. I always wondered how to spot these herbs until someone told me that you often don't – you smell them instead. A subtle garlic smell filling the woods indicates a wild garlic field nearby. Just one word of warning: wild garlic often grows alongside lily of the valley. Their leaves look very similar, but the lilies' leaves are toxic so don't mix them up! If you're not sure, scratch or crunch the leaves – if they smell of garlic, they're the right ones!

WILD GARLIC SOUP

❀ Serves 4 • Prep 40' • Quick & Easy • Vegetarian ❀

1 onion
1 garlic clove
4 courgettes
2 tbsp olive oil
1l vegetable stock
100g wild garlic +
  extra to serve
1 tbsp mint, chopped
lemon juice, to taste
salt and pepper

To serve:
soft goat's cheese with
  wild garlic
croutons

Peel and chop the onion. Peel and crush the garlic clove.

Trim the courgettes, halve lengthwise, then cut into slices.

Heat the olive oil in a large saucepan and fry the onion for 4 minutes until soft, add the garlic and fry for another minute.

Add the courgette slices and fry for a couple of minutes, then add the vegetable stock, cover and bring to the boil. Reduce the heat and simmer for 10 minutes until the courgettes are soft.

Meanwhile, wash and pat dry the wild garlic and chop.

Once the courgettes are soft, remove the saucepan from the heat. Add the wild garlic and mint and blend with a hand blender until smooth.

Adjust the seasoning with salt, pepper and lemon juice.

Serve each portion of soup with some soft goat's cheese and croutons, and sprinkle with a bit of chopped wild garlic.

TIPS

• This soup also tastes great topped with a wild garlic pesto. Just blitz 2 handfuls of wild garlic with 15g of pine nuts, 20g of Parmesan cheese, ½ garlic clove, 40ml of olive oil and a pinch of salt.

• If it's not in season you can replace the wild garlic with spinach leaves or chard.

Luxembourg is a country that loves potatoes, and I can't imagine any local village fête, BBQ or buffet without a generous bowl of hearty potato salad. Traditionally, potato salad is smothered in a thick coating of mayonnaise and served with *Wirschtecher* (sausages) – much to the delight of most children, who tend to get a *Rëndelchen* (a sausage slice) to eat on the spot at the butcher's counter when their parents shop for meat. To give this classic Luxembourg salad a little twist I have thrown in plenty of fragrant herbs, so the mayonnaise turns green and more refreshing and zingy in taste.

GREEN POTATO SALAD WITH SAUSAGES

❤ Serves 4 • Prep 1h • Cooling 30' • Easy ❤

800g waxy potatoes
3 pickled gherkins
3 tsp capers
1 shallot

For the mayonnaise:
2 egg yolks
2 tsp mustard + extra
   to serve
200ml sunflower oil
1 tsp white wine
   vinegar
½ bunch parsley
½ bunch chervil
1 bunch tarragon
salt and pepper

8 small Frankfurter
   sausages or 4 large
   ones
crispy fried onions,
   to serve
mustard, to serve

Start by preparing the potato salad. Wash the potatoes and put into a saucepan with salted water. Cover, bring to the boil and cook for 25 minutes until soft.

Drain the potatoes and rinse under a cold running tap. Peel the potatoes while still hot, quarter, slice and put into a bowl. Leave to cool completely.

Finely chop the gherkins and capers and add to the bowl. Peel and finely chop the shallot and add to the bowl.

To make the mayonnaise, put the egg yolks and mustard into a bowl and beat with an electric whisk. Slowly add the sunflower oil in a thin, steady stream while beating vigorously. Season with the vinegar, and salt and pepper.

Put all the herbs into a blender and finely chop. Add the mayonnaise and blend into a herby mayonnaise.

Add the mayonnaise to the potatoes and mix. Season generously with salt and pepper.

Heat a saucepan with boiling water. Take off the heat, add the sausages and heat through for 5 minutes.

Distribute the potato salad on 4 plates, sprinkle with crispy fried onions, snuggle 2 sausages next to the salad and add a dollop of mustard.

TIPS

• It's quite easy to burn your fingers peeling the potatoes – my friend Laura gave me a great tip which she learnt in culinary school: crunch up a piece of foil and use it to hold the hot potato.

• The green mayonnaise is also great served as a sauce for pan-fried or grilled fish.

I grew up with chicory salad, so I simply had to include this salad in my book, though it is a slight variation of my mum's version. The reason is that I fell in love with Stilton when I lived in the UK. Stilton is a British blue cheese that's distinctively crumbly, making it the perfect cheese to scatter over salads. Upon my return to Luxembourg, I was so happy to find Stilton widely available in local supermarkets that I instantly started adding it to my mum's classic chicory salad.

CHICORY SALAD WITH WALNUTS & BLUE CHEESE

❧ Serves 4-6 • Prep 30' • Quick & Easy • Vegetarian ❧

For the dressing:
3 tsp mustard
3 tbsp white wine vinegar
6 tbsp sunflower oil
2 tbsp cream
salt and pepper

80g walnuts
6 small chicory heads
2 apples
120g Stilton or blue cheese

Start by making the dressing: in a small bowl, mix the mustard with the white wine vinegar. Gradually add the sunflower oil while stirring, then add the cream and season with salt and pepper. Set aside.

In a dry frying pan, roast the walnuts over a medium heat until fragrant. Set aside to cool.

Slice the chicory heads lengthwise, trim off the bottoms and cut out the inner, triangular core – this is the bitter part of the chicory. Slice and put into a salad bowl. Add the dressing and toss the salad.

Peel and core the apples, then cut into small, bite sized pieces. Add to the chicory.

Roughly chop the walnuts and add to the salad.

Crumble the blue cheese over the salad, toss so that everything is evenly mixed and serve immediately.

 TIP

You could add a few crispy bacon lardons to the salad to make it more filling.

This light carrot salad is infused with the subtle Japanese flavours of ginger and sesame oil. It makes for a refreshing side to the lemongrass côtelettes page 164 or to the okonomiyaki pancake page 102.

JAPANESE CARROT SALAD

❧ Serves 4 as a side • Prep 15' • Marinating 30' • Easy • Vegetarian ❧

450g carrots
2 spring onions
2 tsp ginger, grated
4 tbsp rice wine
   vinegar
salt
4 tbsp sunflower oil
2 tbsp sesame oil
2 tsp sugar
2 tsp black sesame
   seeds

Peel, trim and finely grate the carrots. Put into a serving bowl.

Wash and trim the spring onions and finely slice. Add to the carrots.

In a small bowl, mix the grated ginger, rice wine vinegar and a pinch of salt. Add the sunflower oil, sesame oil and sugar. Pour the dressing over the carrot salad, toss and leave to marinate for 30 minutes.

After 30 minutes, sprinkle with black sesame seeds and serve.

TIP

For a spicy variation you can mix some wasabi into a few dollops of mayonnaise and stir it through the salad.

Attend any barbecue in Luxembourg, and you're sure to come across pasta salad! To be honest, I'm not a fan of our *Nuddelszalot* – overcooked pasta shapes with canned peas and other unidentifiable vegetable chunks, smothered in mayonnaise... Nope, no thanks! That's why I've created this Spanish-inspired alternative. It's basically a paella-style salad made with rice-shaped orzo pasta and studded with crispy, lemony chorizo morsels.

SPANISH PASTA SALAD

❈ Serves 4 • Prep 45' • Cooling 30' • Easy ❈

500ml hot chicken stock
pinch saffron threads
240g orzo pasta
2 tbsp olive oil
130g frozen peas
120g chorizo
juice of ½ lemon
165g roasted peppers, from a jar
50g green or black olives, pitted
4 tbsp parsley, chopped
2 tbsp sherry vinegar
salt and pepper

Put the hot chicken stock and the saffron threads into a saucepan and leave to steep for 2 minutes.

Turn on the heat to high and bring the liquid to the boil. Add the orzo pasta and cook for approximately 8 minutes, stirring from time to time, until all the liquid has been absorbed and the orzo is al dente. Mix in 1 tablespoon of olive oil and set aside to cool for at least 30 minutes.

Meanwhile, cook the peas in boiling salted water for approximately 3 minutes. Drain and run under a cold tap, then put into a salad bowl.

Cut the chorizo into slices, then halve each slice. Fry the chorizo in a dry frying pan until the fat starts to ooze out. Add the lemon juice and fry until the chorizo starts to brown and turn crispy. Add to the bowl with the peas.

Cut the peppers into strips, chop the olives and add both to the bowl.

Add the cooled orzo and the parsley to the salad bowl, toss and add the remaining tablespoon of oil and sherry vinegar. Season with salt and pepper and serve.

TIPS

• If you prefer this salad to be vegetarian, use vegetable stock and replace the chorizo with halloumi.
• This salad goes well with a dollop of sriracha mayonnaise from page 98.

Beetroot salad is a classic at any salad buffet in Luxembourg. I have decided to jazz it up by adding avocado and a dressing with a slight wasabi kick.

BEETROOT & AVOCADO SALAD

❧ Serves 4 as a side • Prep 20' • Quick & Easy • Vegetarian ❧

500g cooked beetroot
1 avocado
juice of ½ lemon
1 tbsp black sesame
seeds, to serve

For the dressing:
1 tsp wasabi
2 tbsp mayonnaise
1 tbsp rice wine vinegar
1 tbsp sunflower oil
salt and pepper

Cut the beetroot into cubes and put into a bowl.

Halve the avocado, remove the stone and peel. Cut into cubes and add to the bowl together with the lemon juice.

Mix all the dressing ingredients and pour over the salad; toss so everything is evenly coated.

Sprinkle with sesame seeds and serve.

TIP

You can replace the wasabi with Dijon mustard and the rice wine vinegar with white wine vinegar for a less exotic version.

Cucumber salad is a classic at mine, usually dressed with a simple cream-based vinaigrette (like on page 85) with some fresh dill. I think that is what most Luxembourgers have in mind when they think cucumber salad. However, lately I have taken to pairing cucumbers with exciting Thai flavours – they are a perfect match and this salad is a superb way to jazz up the summer salad buffet.

THAI-STYLE CUCUMBER SALAD

❀ Serves 4 • Prep 30' • Easy ❀

2 cucumbers
1 red chilli
2 tbsp coconut
    shavings
2 tbsp peanuts
2 tbsp coriander,
    chopped
2 tbsp mint, chopped
2 tbsp crispy onions

For the dressing:
2 tbsp tamarind puree
2 tsp lime juice
2 tbsp Thai fish sauce
2 tbsp palm sugar or
    soft brown sugar
1 shallot
1 garlic clove

Peel the cucumbers and halve lengthwise. Scrape out the seeds with a spoon and discard. Cut the cucumbers into cubes and put into a bowl.

Destem the chilli, slice open lengthwise, remove the seeds and finely chop. Add to the bowl.

Heat a dry frying pan and toast the coconut shavings until golden. Set aside. In the same pan, toast the peanuts until fragrant. Set aside.

Make the dressing: in a bowl, mix the tamarind, lime juice, fish sauce and sugar. Peel and finely chop the shallot, peel and crush the garlic and add to the dressing.

Pour the dressing over the salad and toss with the chopped herbs until everything is evenly coated.

Just before serving, sprinkle each portion with coconut shavings, peanuts and crispy onions.

TIP

If you can get hold of fresh Thai basil, add it to the salad as it makes this dish even more complex and refreshing!

Red cabbage is a very popular winter vegetable in Luxembourg. My mum would always make a big pot of braised red cabbage with apples that she would serve as a side to roast meats on Sundays. During my time in the UK I fell in love with raw cabbage, mainly thanks to mayonnaise-laced coleslaw. Every winter I would play around with slaw flavours and this one is a strong favourite, combining exotic mango and pomegranate seeds with fragrant herbs and a sweet and sour dressing. It's definitely no traditional Luxembourg dish, but a nod to the red cabbage season at home nevertheless.

RED WINTER SLAW

Serves 6 • Prep 55' • Marinating 1h • A little effort • Vegetarian

For the dressing:
100ml lime juice
  (2-3 limes)
1 tsp grated ginger
4 tbsp maple syrup
2 tsp soy sauce
¼ tsp dried chilli flakes
1 tbsp mango chutney
2 tbsp sesame oil
3 tbsp sunflower oil

For the salad:
½ red cabbage (500g)
1 mango
½ pomegranate
1 red chilli
5 spring onions
1 bunch of mint
1 bunch of coriander
flaked almonds,
  to serve
crispy fried onions,
  to serve

Put all the dressing ingredients except for the sunflower oil into a little saucepan and bring to the boil. Cook for 10 minutes until the liquid has reduced to a slightly syrupy consistency. Pour into a small bowl and add the sunflower oil. Leave to cool.

Meanwhile, finely slice the red cabbage in a food processor or with a mandolin. Put into a large bowl.

Peel the mango and cut the flesh off the stone. Cut into bite-sized slices and add to the cabbage.

Remove the seeds from the pomegranate and add to the cabbage.

Destem the chilli, slice open lengthwise, remove the seeds and finely chop. Trim the spring onions and finely slice. Chop the mint and the coriander and add to the bowl.

Pour the cooled dressing over the slaw and mix well.

Leave to macerate for at least 1 hour before serving; this will infuse the flavours and soften the cabbage.

Before serving, roast the flaked almonds in a dry frying pan until golden.

Distribute the slaw between 6 plates and sprinkle with flaked almonds and crispy fried onions.

TIP

The least messy way to get the seeds out of a pomegranate is to submerge the pomegranate in a bowl with cold water and remove the seeds under water. Drain and remove any white pith that may still stick to the seeds.

Let me introduce you to your new favourite Luxembourg lunchbox filler!
A soft tortilla wrap folded around a delicious meat salad and tasty quinoa, drizzled with garlicky yoghurt mayonnaise. For those not yet in the know, *Feierstengszalot* is a classic meat salad from Luxembourg. It literally translates as 'Flintstone salad', probably because there are not many vegetables involved in this carnivore's delight. It works wonders in this wrap and I am sure all your colleagues will envy you for your one-of-a-kind lunchtime treat.

FEIERSTENGSZALOT WRAPS

❋ Makes 6 wraps • Prep 30' • Cooking 2h30'• Cooling 2h15' • Marinating overnight • A little effort ❋

For the Feierstengszalot:
500g chuck (paleron)
1 small carrot
1 small leek
1 bay leaf
3 peppercorns
1 tbsp coarse salt

100g quinoa
1 egg
15 cherry tomatoes
2 pickled gherkins
½ iceberg lettuce
4 tbsp mayonnaise
150g yoghurt
1 garlic clove
6 tortilla wraps

Put the meat, carrot, leek, bay leaf, peppercorns and coarse salt into a large saucepan. Add 1l of water, bring to the boil, then reduce the heat, cover and simmer for 2 ½ hours, until the meat is tender.

After 2 ½ hours, remove the meat from the saucepan and leave to cool for 15 minutes. Strain the cooking liquid and set aside; discard the vegetables.

After 15 minutes, put the meat into a container and leave in the fridge for at least 1 hour.

Meanwhile prepare the salad dressing (page 85).

Rinse the quinoa in a sieve under a running tap. Put into a saucepan with 230ml of the cooking liquid from the meat. Cover and bring to the boil, then cook for 12 minutes. Uncoverand cook for another 5 minutes until all the liquid has been absorbed. Set aside.

Take the meat out of the fridge and cut into small cubes. Put the meat back into the container, add the dressing and mix until the meat is well covered. Close the container and pop back into the fridge for at least 1 hour (or overnight).

Meanwhile, boil the egg for 10 minutes and rinse under cold water. Leave to cool for a few minutes, peel and cut into small cubes. Quarter the cherry tomatoes. Cut the gherkins into little slices. Add everything to the meat and mix.

Chop the iceberg lettuce. Mix the mayonnaise and yoghurt in a small bowl. Peel and crush the garlic and mix with the yoghurt mayonnaise; season with salt and pepper.

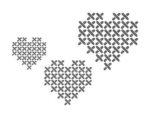

Microwave a tortilla wrap for 5-10 seconds to make it softer and easier to fold. Lay the tortilla out in front of you and put a handful of chopped iceberg lettuce in the centre, leaving a 3 cm border on each side. Top the salad with quinoa, then drizzle with the yoghurt mayonnaise. Top with Feierstengszalot and finish by adding some more lettuce on top.

Fold in the left and right sides of the tortilla, then roll the bottom edge of the tortilla over the filling, tucking it into the wrap. Make 5 more wraps with the remaining ingredients.

Cut the wraps in half and serve.

 TIP   You can prepare the *Feierstengszalot* up to 2 days in advance.

MY FAVOURITE SALAD DRESSING

2 tsp mustard
2 tbsp white wine
  vinegar
4 tbsp sunflower oil
1 tsp dried salad herbs
3 tsp cream
salt and pepper

In a small bowl combine all the ingredients for the salad dressing until they arere evenly mixed, then season with salt and pepper.

A popular autumnal starter in Luxembourg is *Toast aux Champignons* – a slice of toasted bread topped with creamy mushrooms. It's a really simple yet incredibly satisfying dish and I absolutely love it. This is a completely wacky take on the classic – a pillowy bread bun stuffed with mushrooms and served with a creamy mushroom dipping sauce. The inspiration for this recipe comes from soft Chinese dumplings, often referred to as *baos*, which are usually stuffed with pork. I've decided to make them vegetarian and to use the classic *Toast aux Champignons* topping. The buns are in fact a bit of a cheat's version, as I use baking powder instead of yeast to make them rise a lot faster. That way you can fill the buns instantly and start steaming, no patience required.

STEAMED MUSHROOM BUNS

❀ Makes 12 buns • Prep 1h15' • A little effort • Vegetarian ❀

750g chestnut
  mushrooms
3 shallots
3 garlic cloves
50g butter
50ml white wine
150ml cream
salt and pepper
sesame seeds, to serve

For the buns:
300g flour
3 tsp baking powder
200ml milk
¼ tsp salt

Clean the mushrooms and roughly chop them in batches in a food processor. Set aside.

Peel and finely chop the shallots. Peel and crush the garlic.

Melt the butter in a large frying pan. Fry the shallots for 4 minutes until soft, add the garlic and fry for another minute.

Add half of the chopped mushrooms and a pinch of salt and fry over a high heat, stirring regularly, until the mushrooms have released all their juices. Keep frying until the liquid has been absorbed. Put into a bowl, then fry the remaining mushrooms without adding any butter.

Once you have fried all the mushrooms, season them with salt and pepper and set aside.

Make the bun dough: with an electric whisk, mix the flour, baking powder, milk and salt until the dough comes together. Knead with your hands for 2 more minutes until you have a smooth dough. Roll into a log and cut into 12 equal-sized pieces.

With your hands, flatten a piece of dough into a disc, place a heaped teaspoon of mushroom filling into the centre, then fold and pull the edges up over the filling and pinch together so the dumpling is sealed.

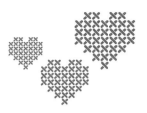

Put the dumplings onto a piece of baking paper, seal side down, and place into a bamboo steamer. Repeat with the remaining dough.

Stack the bamboo steamers on top of each other and top with a lid. Put into a large wok or frying pan over a high heat. Pour some boiling water into the bottom of the wok – it's important that the water level is lower than the platform on which the dumplings sit, to make sure the dumplings are steamed and not boiled. Steam the buns for 8 minutes.

Halfway through the steaming process, sprinkle the buns with sesame seeds and steam for the remaining time.

While the dumplings are steaming, finish the mushroom sauce. Put the remaining fried mushrooms back into the frying pan and heat through. Add the white wine and cook for a couple of minutes, then add the cream and bring to the boil. Take off the heat and adjust the seasoning with salt and pepper.

Serve the steamed buns with mushroom sauce and a green salad.

• You can get bamboo steaming baskets in most supermarkets and in every Asian shop. I would recommend buying a few baskets of the same size and only one lid, as you can stack the baskets to steam up to 3 'levels' at the same time. My baskets have a diameter of 20cm and they fit 5 dumplings.

• If you have a steam oven, you can cook the dumplings in there for 8 minutes at 100°C.

• The mushroom sauce also works as a simple and tasty pasta sauce, especially if you add some Parmesan shavings at the end.

My love affair with green asparagus began in the UK, where you hardly ever find white asparagus. These toasts pair the smokiness of chargrilled green asparagus with salty bacon and creamy goat's cheese. A delightful treat!

ASPARAGUS TOASTS WITH GOAT'S CHEESE

❀ Serves 2 • Prep 30' • Quick & Easy ❀

250g green asparagus
1 tbsp olive oil
8 slices of smoked bacon
4 slices of sourdough bread
120g soft goat's cheese with chives
salt and pepper

Wash the asparagus and trim off the tough ends. Toss the asparagus in 1 tablespoon of olive oil.

Heat a griddle pan or a barbecue and grill the asparagus for 7 to 15 minutes (depending on thickness), turning them regularly so that they get lightly charred on all sides and they are cooked through. Season with salt and pepper.

Meanwhile, fry the bacon in a frying pan until crispy, drain on kitchen paper.

Toast the sourdough bread and spread some soft goats' cheese on top.

Arrange a few asparagus spears on top and finish with 2 slices of bacon.

TIPS

• For a vegetarian version you could replace the bacon with some toasted pine nuts or walnuts.

• I tend to pick thin spears for grilling, as they will soften quite quickly.

I'm fairly sure all Luxembourgers love waffles – they are served at every village fête and they are definitely one of the highlights at the annual fun fair in the capital, the *Schueberfouer*. A classic Luxembourg *Eisekuch* is dusted with icing sugar or topped with whipped cream and strawberry slices. When it comes to the batter though, there are many variations: some people use sparkling water, others swear by lemonade or even beer to create the perfect light, aerated waffle. I just whip my egg whites until stiff and fold them into the batter – it makes for a slightly chewier waffle that is light at the same time. I have taken some liberty with the savoury topping here – pesto whipped cream and roast tomatoes is definitely an odd one, but the combination has wowed anyone who has ever tried it! Either way, my batter works for both sweet and savoury toppings!

DUO OF GAUFRES

❋ Makes 10 waffles • Prep 1h • Resting 1h • Easy • Vegetarian ❋

For the waffles:
3 eggs
125ml cream
250ml milk
125g butter, melted
250g flour
½ tsp salt

For the savoury topping:
250g cherry tomatoes
40ml olive oil + extra
  for the tomatoes
herbes de Provence
1 bunch of basil
15g pine nuts
½ garlic clove
20g Parmesan
150ml cream
salt and pepper
sunflower oil,
  for greasing
Parmesan shavings,
  to serve

For the sweet topping:
Icing sugar
Cinnamon

Start by making the waffle batter: Separate the eggs and whisk the egg whites with a pinch of salt until stiff.

In another bowl, whisk the egg yolks with the cream and the milk.
Add the melted butter and salt and whisk again.

Put the flour into a large bowl and gradually add the liquid ingredients while whisking. Fold in the stiff egg whites until you get an even, aerated batter. Set aside and leave to rest at room temperature for 1 hour.

Meanwhile, prepare the toppings: Preheat the oven to 180°C fan. Put the tomatoes into a roasting tin, drizzle with some olive oil, season with herbes de Provence and salt and pepper. Roast in the preheated oven for 12 minutes until soft. Take out of the oven, cover with foil to keep warm and set aside.

For the pesto whipped cream: put the basil, pine nuts, garlic, Parmesan and 40ml olive oil into a blender and pulse into a slightly chunky pesto, refrigerate.

For the sweet topping, mix some icing sugar with cinnamon and set aside.

After 1 hour of resting, grease the waffle iron with some sunflower oil and preheat according to the machine instructions.

Using a ladle, pour some batter into the centre of the waffle iron, close the iron and bake until the waffle is golden (this can take between 2 – 5 minutes).
You can open the iron after a minute or so and fill in the gaps (if there are any) with some more batter. Put the finished waffles onto a wire rack. Repeat with the remaining batter.

Once all the waffles are done put the cream into a bowl and whip stiff. Fold in the pesto and adjust the seasoning with salt and pepper. Put into a piping bag fitted with a star-shaped nozzle. Pipe some pesto onto 5 waffles, top with cherry tomatoes and Parmesan shavings and season with salt and pepper.

Dust the remaining 5 waffles with cinnamon sugar and serve.

Go anywhere for brunch in London or NYC, and you are bound to find avocado toast on the menu – a place is not hip unless it serves it (the hip-list also requires mismatched crockery, exposed brick walls and bearded baristas sporting extravagant tattoos). Some places serve their avocado toast with strawberry slices – admittedly a strange pairing, but somehow it really works. So, when I developed this recipe I thought why not make a strawberry ketchup?! It's definitely pushing the boat out, so if you would rather stay in the flavour safe zone I suggest you use traditional ketchup.

AVOCADO & EGG SCHMIER

❀ Serves 2 • Prep 50' • Cooling 2h • Easy • Vegetarian ❀

1 large ripe avocado or
  2 small ones
juice of ½ lemon
4 slices of sourdough
  bread
olive oil, for brushing
2 eggs
salt and pepper

Start by making the ketchup in advance and leave to cool.

For the toast peel, halve and destone the avocado. Cut into chunks, put into a bowl and roughly mash with a fork. Drizzle with a bit of lemon juice and season with salt and pepper. Cover the surface with cling film, so that no air stays between the avocado and the cling film.

Cut a hole into 2 of the bread slices – you can use a cookie cutter, a serving ring or a glass to do so. Discard the bread discs. Brush the 4 bread slices with olive oil on each side.

Heat a frying pan and fry the bread slices without the hole for a few minutes on one side until crispy. Put them onto two serving plates, crispy side down.

Fry the bread slices with the hole for a few minutes on one side until crispy. Flip in the pan, crack an egg into each hole, cover the pan with a lid and cook for about 3 minutes until the egg is cooked through.

Meanwhile, spread some strawberry ketchup over the two plated bread slices and top with mashed avocado.

Once the eggs are done, season with salt and pepper and put the eggy bread slices on top of the mashed avocado.

Serve immediately.

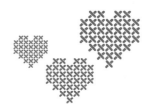

STRAWBERRY KETCHUP

250g strawberries
1 shallot
60ml white wine
   vinegar
40g dark cane sugar
2 tsp Worcestershire
   sauce
½ tsp salt
¼ tsp powdered ginger
¼ tsp smoked paprika
¼ tsp powdered cumin
¼ tsp chilli flakes
   (optional)

Wash, trim and quarter the strawberries. Put into a small saucepan.

Peel and finely chop the shallot and add to the strawberries. Add all the remaining ketchup ingredients, stir and bring to the boil. Cook for 15 minutes until reduced and sticky.

Leave the ketchup to cool for 10 minutes, then blend into a purée with a hand blender. If you prefer a smooth ketchup without any pips, press the purée through a fine-mesh sieve or immediately fill into a jam jar. Leave to cool completely, then refrigerate.

The strawberry ketchup will keep in the fridge in a sealed jar for 2 months.

In Luxembourg we often have corn on the cob at barbecues, simply smothered in butter and sprinkled with salt. I love corn on the cob but I'm not a fan of the nasty fibres that get stuck in your teeth! Therefore, I would like to propose a new way to enjoy barbecued corn: in a taco! These sweetcorn tacos have surprised many of my meat-loving friends, who found themselves saying no to sausages and yes to my veggie tacos...!

SWEETCORN TACOS

❀ Makes 6 tacos • Prep 45' • Easy • Vegetarian ❀

2 corn on the cob,
    uncooked
20g butter, melted
½ red onion
50g mayonnaise
1 tsp sriracha sauce
½ lime
6 mini tortilla wraps
salt

To serve:
iceberg lettuce,
    chopped
100g feta
coriander, chopped

Light the barbecue and wait until it's at a medium heat; this should take about 30 minutes. You can tell it's ready when the embers are glowing.

Remove the husks, if there are any, from the corn on the cob, wash and pat dry. Place each cob on a piece of foil and brush all over with melted butter. Sprinkle with salt and wrap the cobs in the foil.

Put the corn parcels on the barbecue and grill for 20 minutes, turning regularly.

While the corn is on the barbecue, prepare the rest. Finely chop the red onion and set aside. In a small bowl, mix the mayonnaise with the sriracha.

After 20 minutes, take the corn off the barbecue and remove the foil. Put back on the barbecue and grill for another few minutes, turning regularly so the corn gets some char marks.

Place a small bowl upside down into a wide mixing bowl so that it sits inside the bowl like a cupola. Place one corn on the cob upwards on the base of the small bowl and cut down along the length of the cob so that the corn kernels fall into the bowl. Alternatively, place the corn on the cob on a chopping board and shave the kernels off on there; this will be messier though, as the kernels tend to spill everywhere.

Remove the small bowl and mix the corn kernels with the chopped red onion. Add the juice of half a lime, the sriracha mayonnaise and sprinkle with salt. Mix until the kernels are evenly coated.

Put the tortilla wraps on the barbecue and grill for a few seconds on both sides.

Put the tortilla wraps onto plates and top each with a bit of salad and corn kernels. Crumble some feta over each tortilla, then top with some chopped coriander.

 TIP   Add some fried chorizo slices if you prefer to have a bit of meat with these tacos.

This is a super quick and easy recipe, perfect for a speedy lunch, dinner in a hurry or for a lazy Sunday brunch. To make it more filling, serve the omelette with some quinoa or toasted whole-wheat bread on the side.

COURGETTE OMELETTE WITH MINT & FETA

❖ Makes 1 omelette • Prep 20' • Easy • Vegetarian ❖

½ courgette
2 spring onions
10g butter
1 garlic clove
2 tbsp mint, chopped
4 eggs
2 tbsp cream
20g feta
salt and pepper

Grate the courgette. Trim the spring onions and cut into slices.

Melt the butter in a frying pan of approximately 15cm. Fry the grated courgette for 2 minutes.

Peel and crush the garlic clove and add it to the courgettes with the mint and spring onions. Fry for another minute.

In a bowl, beat the eggs and the cream together and season with salt and pepper. Add the egg mix to the frying pan and crumble the feta on top.

Cook the omelette over a medium heat. Allow the egg to set a little, then, using a wooden spoon, gently drag the egg away from the edges toward the centre of the pan, allowing the uncooked egg to flow behind the cooked egg.

When most of the omelette is cooked, fold the omelette in half, slide onto a plate and serve immediately with a green side salad.

TIP

Why not try the following omelette fillings:
• Garlic mushrooms, tarragon and brie
• Bacon, onion, thyme and cheddar
• Smoked salmon, chives and cream cheese
• Sundried tomato, olives and artichokes

In the summer of 2015, I was in Tokyo to cook for the National Day reception at the Luxembourg embassy. Whenever I wasn't standing in the kitchen or hunting down European ingredients for my finger food banquet, I was eating my way around this exciting city. In particular, I loved spending my evenings in tiny little restaurants that prepare *okonomiyaki* right in front of you. *Okonomiyaki* is a very popular Japanese cabbage pancake from Hiroshima and Osaka. It is fried and then smothered in a lip-smacking *okonomiyaki* sauce, then drizzled with mayonnaise and sprinkled with dried tuna flakes. I've tweaked the recipe a little bit by using ingredients that are easy to find in Luxembourg. This is now my favourite recipe to make use of the abundance of cabbage during our long winters.

OKONOMIYAKI PANCAKE

❧ Makes 2 pancakes • Prep 50' • Easy ❧

For the sauce:
1 garlic clove
4 tbsp ketchup
2 tbsp soy sauce
1 tbsp white wine
1 ½ tbsp sugar
1 tbsp white wine
   vinegar
½ tsp ginger, grated
½ tsp mustard
2 tbsp water

For the pancakes:
150g savoy cabbage
150g potato
2 spring onions
100g flour
1 tbsp soy sauce
2 tbsp ginger, grated
2 eggs
100ml cold
   vegetable stock
2 tbsp sunflower oil

To serve:
Mayonnaise
Nori seaweed strips
Bonito flakes (optional)
1 spring onion,
   chopped

Start by making the okonomiyaki sauce: Peel and crush the garlic. Put all the ingredients into a small saucepan and bring to the boil. Cook for 10 minutes until the sauce has thickened. Set aside until needed.

Roughly chop the cabbage, peel and grate the potato, trim and slice the spring onions and put everything into a bowl.

Add the flour, soy sauce, ginger, eggs and stock and mix until you get a homogeneous batter.

Heat 1 tablespoon of sunflower oil in a frying pan, add half the batter and form a pancake approximately 20 cm in width and 1.5 cm in height.

Fry the pancake for 4 minutes on one side until golden, flip and cook for another 4 minutes on the other side.

Slide the pancake onto a plate, brush the top with half the okonomiyaki sauce, drizzle with mayonnaise, sprinkle with nori strips and bonito flakes (if using) and chopped spring onions.

Repeat with the remaining batter to make a second pancake.

 TIPS

• Bonito flakes are dried tuna flakes. They look and smell like fish food, but trust me, they have an incredible taste and add a unique smokiness to this dish. It will blow your mind! They also come with quite the show-stopping effect, as the heat of the *okonomiyaki* will make the delicate flakes 'dance' and move on top. You can find bonito flakes in Asian shops. Store them in an airtight container.
• For a more filling version you can cover the top of the unbaked pancake with bacon strips in the pan before flipping it over.

If you have ever been to a Luxembourg *Kiermes*, you will have come across, and hopefully tasted, *Gromperekichelcher*, deep-fried potato cakes that are served with apple compote. My absolute favourite! What if there was a way to make them even better? Say by stuffing melted cheese and smoky ham between two (!) *Gromperekichelcher*? Total indulgence – yes please! Plus, it's super quick and easy to make, the perfect hangover food for a lazy Sunday morning. I like to use Luxembourg *Bauerenham* in this recipe, as its taste is the perfect match for this hearty dish.

GROMPEREKICHELCHER CORDON BLEU

❧ Makes 2 Cordon Bleu • Prep 20' • Easy ❧

500g floury potatoes
½ tsp salt
groundnut oil,
  for frying
50g Berdorfer Roude
  Bouf cheese, grated
1 large slice of cooked
  ham

apple compote,
  to serve

Peel the potatoes and finely grate them. Season with salt, put into a sieve over a bowl and press out as much liquid as you can.

Pour enough groundnut oil into a frying pan for the entire bottom of the pan to be covered. Heat the oil and test if the oil is hot enough by dropping a tiny bit of grated potato into the oil – if it starts bubbling, you're good to go. Drop half of the potato mix into the pan to make 2 Gromperekichelcher, flatten and fry on each side for about 2 to 3 minutes. Take out of the pan and put onto a plate lined with kitchen paper, to absorb some of the grease.

Continue with the remaining batter and make 2 more potato cakes. Fry on one side for 2 minutes, flip over and top the fried sides with ¼ of the grated cheese, half a slice of ham and the remaining cheese, then top with the Gromperekichelcher that you fried earlier.

Keep frying for 2 minutes, so that the cheese melts and the bottoms of the Gromperekichelcher become crispy.

Serve straight out of the pan with a dollop of apple compote and a green salad.

TIP

A traditional *Gromperekichelchen* is made with egg, onion, flour and parsley – if you want to give it a try, grate 2 potatoes and 1 onion, add 1 egg, 2 tbsp flour, ½ tsp salt and 1 tsp chopped parsley. Mix and leave to rest for 30 minutes. You need to stir the batter again before frying as it will have drawn out quite a bit of liquid.

This 'tart' is quite a revelation. The base is completely flourless, and made using cauliflower, ground almonds and egg instead. This concept is often referred to as 'cauliflower crust pizza' and has caused a real craze in the health blogosphere. Let me be frank though, the gluten-free base tastes nothing like a traditional pizza dough. Instead it provides this tart with a light and crumbly base, and a lovely nutty flavour. As to what goes on top: feel free to throw your favourite pizza toppings on the base; anything goes really! Oh, and if you have fussy kids, this recipe is a sneaky way to hide some healthy vegetables in one of their favourite dishes.

CAULIFLOWER FLAMMKUCHEN

❖ Makes 2 tarts of approx. 25 cm • Prep 25' • Oven 35' • Easy ❖

For the cauliflower base:
1 cauliflower (about 800g, trimmed)
100g ground almonds
2 eggs
salt and pepper
sunflower oil, to grease

For the topping:
180g crème fraîche
½ onion
60g Bio-Haff Baltes Routgewäschenen 'Mëll Gees' cheese or Munster
60g bacon lardons
salt and pepper

Preheat the oven to 180°C fan.

Discard the cauliflower leaves and cut the cauliflower into small pieces. Put into a food processor and whizz until the cauliflower is very finely chopped and resembles couscous grains.

Put the chopped cauliflower into a bowl and microwave for 5 minutes at 800W. Tip the microwaved cauliflower onto a clean tea towel and leave to cool for 5 minutes.

Wrap the tea towel around the cauliflower and squeeze out as much liquid as you can, then put back into the bowl. Add the almonds and eggs to the cauliflower, season with salt and pepper and mix well.

Line two baking trays with baking paper and grease with some sunflower oil. Divide the cauliflower mix in two and put one heap onto each baking tray. Shape with your hands into a disc 1cm thick.

Bake the bases in the preheated oven for 25 minutes.

Meanwhile, season the crème fraîche with salt and pepper. Peel and finely slice the onion. Cut the cheese into cubes.

After 25 minutes, take the cauliflower bases out of the oven. Spread each base with the seasoned crème fraîche and top with onions, cheese and bacon lardons.

Bake for another 10 minutes so the cheese melts. Serve with a green salad.

TIPS

• If you don't have a microwave you can skip this step and use the raw chopped cauliflower instead. Bake the plain base 10 minutes longer, so 35 minutes in total. The tart will be much wetter though, as the cauliflower will release its water in the oven.

• For a veggie *Flamm'*, replace the bacon lardons with smoked scamorza cheese.

Since moving back to Luxembourg I have noticed a growing interest in seasonal and regional food and produce. Many people now seem to be aware of what they eat when, and of where their food comes from – so when the Luxembourg non-profit organization SOS Faim approached me to create a springtime recipe with regional produce for their 'Changeons de Menu' campaign, I was all in. I came up with this beautiful vegetarian quiche, and I liked it so much that I decided to include it here.

CARROT QUICHE WITH GOAT'S CHEESE

❧ Makes 1 quiche of approx. 23cm • Prep 30' • Fridge 2h • Oven 45' • Easy • Vegetarian ❧

For the pastry:
150g spelt flour
½ tsp salt
60g butter + extra for
  greasing
1 egg
a splash of water

For the filling:
50g wheat grains
  (Ebly)
170ml vegetable stock
2 carrots
8 spring onions
250ml cream
3 eggs
½ tsp salt
pepper
1 tbsp mustard
100g soft goat's
  cheese log

Start by making the pastry: put the flour and salt into a bowl. Cut the butter into cubes and add to the flour. Rub the butter and flour between your hands until it resembles breadcrumbs. Add the egg and water and knead into a dough.

Shape the dough into a disc, wrap in cling film and chill in the fridge for at least 2 hours.

Meanwhile, cook the wheat grains in the vegetable stock for 10 minutes until all the liquid has been absorbed. Set aside.

Peel and grate the carrots. Trim the spring onions and finely slice.

In a jug, mix the cream with the eggs, salt and pepper.

Butter a 23cm quiche tin.

After 2 hours, take the dough out of the fridge and preheat the oven to 180°C fan.

Unwrap the dough and place it onto a surface dusted with flour. Roll into a thin disc slightly bigger than the quiche form. Lift the dough into the tin and press it firmly against the rim to make it stick. Cut off any excess pastry.

Brush the pastry bottom with mustard.

Put the grated carrot, spring onion slices and cooked wheat berries into the quiche tin. Pour the egg cream onto the vegetables.

Slice the goat's cheese and place on top of the quiche.

Bake in the preheated oven for 45 minutes. Serve with a green salad.

I know there are many *Träipen* skeptics out there, but this quiche has managed to win over every single one of them so far! All the sides traditionally served with a *Träip* are thrown into a crisp spelt pastry, and come out of the oven as one seriously delicious quiche. Simply awesome!

TRÄIPEN QUICHE

❀ Makes 1 quiche of 30cm or 2 of 20cm • Serves 6 • Prep 40' • Cooling 2h • Oven 1h • Easy ❀

For the pastry:
250g spelt flour + extra for dusting
1 tsp salt
125g cold butter + extra for greasing
1 egg
35ml cold water

For the filling:
350g jar of ready-to-eat braised red cabbage
2 tbsp mustard
2 Träipen sausages or black pudding
350g jar of chunky apple compote
2 eggs
100ml cream
salt and pepper

Start by making the pastry: put the flour and salt into a bowl. Cut the butter into cubes and add to the flour. Rub the butter and flour between your fingers until it resembles breadcrumbs. Add the egg and water and knead into a dough.

Shape the pastry into a disc, wrap in cling film and chill in the fridge for at least 2 hours.

Grease the quiche tin and set aside.

After 2 hours, preheat the oven to 180°C fan.

Put the red cabbage into a sieve and leave to drain.

Unwrap the chilled pastry and place it on a work surface dusted with flour. Roll into a very thin disc that's slightly bigger than the quiche tin. Lift the dough into the tin and press it firmly against the rim to make it stick. Cut off any excess pastry.

Brush the pastry base with the mustard.

Slit each Träip skin lengthwise, remove the sausage meat and discard the skin. Cut the meat into small chunks, put into a bowl and roughly mash with a fork. Top the mustard-covered pastry with the mashed Träip.

Top the Träip with a layer of apple compote.

Top the apple compote with the red cabbage.

In a bowl, beat the eggs with the cream and season with salt and pepper. Pour over the red cabbage and bake the quiche in the preheated oven for 1 hour.

 TIP
If you're feeling lazy or pressed for time you can of course use ready-made shortcrust pastry.

When I think of chicory, two dishes from my childhood instantly pop into my mind: chicory salad with apples and walnuts (page 69) and baked chicory with ham in a béchamel sauce (see serving suggestion at the bottom). As a child, I used to find raw chicory much too bitter, but I absolutely loved it baked – that is because once it is baked, the vegetable loses its bitterness and takes on a moorish buttery flavour. Chicory is also beautiful paired with sweet ingredients: in this recipe I am combining caramelized chicory with salty feta in a flaky puff pastry. A stunning veggie main!

CHICORY TARTE TATIN

❧ 30cm quiche tin • Serves 4 • Prep 40' • Oven 30' • Easy • Vegetarian ❧

2 onions
80g butter
5 chicory heads
3 sprigs of fresh thyme
60g sugar
200g feta
20g pine nuts
230g all-butter
   puff pastry
salt and pepper

Preheat the oven to 200°C fan.

Peel the onions and cut into thin slices. Melt half of the butter in a frying pan and gently fry the onion slices with a pinch of salt for about 10 minutes until really soft.

While the onions are frying, slice open the chicory heads lengthwise and cut out the inner, triangular core – this is the bitter part of the chicory. Set aside. Pull the thyme leaves off the sprigs and set aside.

After 10 minutes, add 1 tablespoon of sugar to the onions and fry for another 5 minutes. Remove the fried onions from the pan and set aside.

Put the remaining sugar into the frying pan and melt over a medium heat, swirling the pan from time to time, but without stirring the sugar. Once the sugar has melted and starts to get a golden hue, add the remaining 40g of butter. Stir until you get a smooth caramel.

Pour the caramel into a 30cm quiche tin, add a pinch of salt, the thyme leaves and the pine nuts. Place the chicory halves cut-side down onto the caramel.

Scatter the onions over the chicory heads and crumble ¾ of the feta on the top. Cover the chicory heads with the puff pastry, tucking in the edges on the side and pricking the pastry with a fork in a few places.

Bake in the preheated oven for 30 minutes.

Once baked, take the tarte tatin out of the oven, turn onto a serving plate, sprinkle with the remaining feta and season with salt and pepper.

Serve with a green salad.

TIP

If you want to make a traditional regional chicory recipe, wrap some cored chicory halves with cooked ham slices, place into an ovenproof dish and cover in béchamel sauce (recipe page 125). Sprinkle with grated cheese and bake in a 200°C fan oven for approximately 30 minutes.

Fondue is one of my favourite winter comfort foods. I can't think of anything cozier and more heartwarming than a saucepan full of melted cheese, spiked with Kirsch! *Kachkéis* is a bit of a Luxembourg food oddity: a cooked cheese that is quite runny – think of the texture of glue: stringy, gloopy and rubbery, but in a good way. In fact, it is a bit like a fondue of sorts! So, to me it was quite obvious that I would have to create a Luxembourg *Kachkéis* fondue! Since *Kachkéis* is usually eaten with mustard, I decided to make some mustardy croutons to go with it – mixing Luxembourgish wholegrain and smooth mustard for the ultimate mustard kick!

KACHKÉIS FONDUE WITH MUSTARD CROUTONS

❀ Serves 4 • Prep 50' • Easy • Vegetarian ❀

For the croutons:
1 ½ baguette
4 ½ tbsp wholegrain mustard
4 ½ tbsp smooth mustard
3 tbsp water
salt

500g uncooked Kachkéis log
200ml white wine
50ml cream
2 garlic cloves
300g Gruyère cheese, grated
pepper
3 tbsp cornstarch
70ml Kirsch

Preheat the oven to 180°C fan.

Cut the baguettes into bite sized pieces and put into a large baking tray.

In a small bowl, mix the mustards with the water and stir until smooth. Pour the mustard over the bread pieces and mix with your hands until the bread is evenly covered. Sprinkle with salt.

Bake in the preheated oven for 15 minutes until crispy, turning the croutons halfway through so that they don't burn.

Cut the Kachkéis log into pieces. Put into a fondue saucepan with the wine and cream and melt, while stirring.

Once the cheese has melted, peel and crush the garlic cloves and add to the Kachkéis with the grated Gruyère and some pepper. Melt into a smooth cheese fondue, stirring constantly.

In a little jar dilute the cornstarch in the Kirsch, add to the cheese fondue and cook for a couple of minutes so the fondue thickens.

Serve the fondue with the mustard croutons and a green salad.

TIPS

• It is always a mess to clean a Fondue saucepan! My trick is to add 1 tablespoon of baking powder and some vinegar to the bottom of the dirty pan and leave to soak for 5 minutes. Then I pour boiling water over it and boil for a few minutes while scraping the bottom with a wooden spatula, watching out that the liquid doesn't boil over! That usually works magic!

• These mustard croutons are also wonderful on a salad. I prefer them a bit more buttery in that case so I replace the water with 75g of melted butter and mix it with the bread cubes before baking them.

The first time I came across the concept of an *aligot*, I was flabbergasted. *Aligot* is a cheesy potato mash from the Aubrac region in the French Massif Central. The recipe asks for copious amounts of Tomme cheese and crème fraîche, which are mixed into mashed potatoes. The result is an indulgent, totally delicious stomach-filler. What makes *aligot* so special is its stringy texture, which reminded me a lot of *Kachkéis* the first time I saw it. People actually hold contests to see who can create the longest *aligot* ribbon. It's cheese madness! This is my Luxembourg answer to *aligot*: made with *Kachkéis* and topped with *Judd* and mustard. It is less stringy than the French version, but it certainly delivers in taste.

KACHKÉIS ALIGOT

❋ Serves 2 as a main or 4 as a starter/side • Prep 1h • Easy ❋

900g floury potatoes
70g butter
2 garlic cloves
250g pot of Kachkéis
   with herbs
2 tbsp sour cream
150g cooked smoked
   pork collar (Judd)
   or cooked ham
salt and pepper

To serve:
parsley
mustard

Wash the potatoes and put into a saucepan with salted water. Cover and bring to the boil and cook for approximately 30 minutes until soft.

Drain and rinse the potatoes under a cold tap. Peel the potatoes while still hot (you can hold the potatoes with a piece of crimpled foil so you don't burn your fingers).

Mash the potatoes and put into a large saucepan.

Melt the butter in a small saucepan. Peel and crush the garlic cloves and add to the melted butter, fry for a minute until fragrant, then add the butter to the mashed potato.

Add the Kachkéis to the mashed potato and put over a medium heat, stirring constantly. Once the cheese is fully incorporated add the sour cream and season with salt and pepper. Set aside and keep warm.

Cut the cooked pork collar into small cubes and fry for a couple of minutes in a dry frying pan, to heat through.

Serve each portion of aligot sprinkled with pork cubes, parsley, a dollop of mustard and a green side salad.

TIP

You can serve this *Kachkéis aligot* (without the pork cubes) as a hearty side dish to a Luxembourg *Wäinzoossiss*.

Asparagus season is my springtime highlight! Unlike in the UK, where green asparagus are the norm, most people in Luxembourg prefer white asparagus. But did you know that they are in fact exactly the same plant? An asparagus can turn green or white depending on how it is grown. When the spears pop out of the ground, they turn green, so in Luxembourg, farmers keep covering the asparagus with soil as they grow upwards, so that they stay white! White asparagus are more delicate in taste than their green siblings, and they need to be peeled, as the skin is quite tough and stringy.

Traditionally, asparagus are served with a Hollandaise sauce, but at home, my mum would always dish up asparagus with a béchamel sauce instead. I was quite surprised when I found out that this is a fairly 'low-fat' béchamel, as most of the liquid is asparagus cooking water, and not cream, as I always thought it was!

ASPARAGUS WITH BÉCHAMEL

❀ Serves 2 • Prep 1h • Easy • Vegetarian ❀

500g white asparagus
600g potatoes
¼ tsp sugar
80g butter
50g flour
100ml cream
a pinch of nutmeg
salt and pepper
chopped parsley,
  to serve

Peel the asparagus and trim off the ends.

Peel the potatoes and cut into quarters. Put into a saucepan with salted water, cover and bring to the boil. Cook for approximately 15 minutes until done. Drain the potatoes, toss in the saucepan with 20g of butter and put on a serving plate.

While the potatoes are boiling, put the asparagus into a saucepan with boiling salted water and the sugar, cover and cook for approximately 20 minutes, until cooked through. Once done, remove 500ml of cooking liquid for the béchamel and leave the asparagus in the saucepan in the remaining hot water.

Make the béchamel just before serving: Melt the remaining 60g butter in a saucepan, add the flour and fry on a medium heat for a couple of minutes until the flour/butter mix starts to turn golden and fragrant.

Gradually add 500ml of the asparagus water, whisking between each addition and leaving it to cook for a minute or so, so that it thickens and you get a smooth sauce.

Then gradually add the cream. Once you have a smooth sauce, season with a pinch of nutmeg and salt and pepper.

Serve the asparagus and potatoes smothered in béchamel and sprinkled with parsley.

TIPS

• You can serve this dish with a few slices of Luxembourgish cooked ham.

• For an asparagus soup reheat any leftover béchamel with a bit of leftover asparagus cooking water. Cut the remaining asparagus and potatoes into bite sized chunks and add to the liquid. Use a hand blender to blend until smooth.

• Asparagus season is also new potato season, so if you can get these little spuds, boil and serve them with the skin on – it's so delicate that you can eat the entire potato.

Gebootschte Gromperen - potatoes pan-fried in heaps of lard and bacon - are a hearty side to many Luxembourg meat dishes. I've been told that in the olden days, people used to pour some coffee over the finished dish, as a sauce of some kind. I prefer to keep it simple and caffeine-free, and serve my *Gebootschte Gromperen* with a fried egg on top.

GEBOOTSCHTE POTATOES WITH A FRIED EGG

Serves 2 • Prep 1h 15' • Cooling 1h • Easy

1kg waxy potatoes
50g lard + 1 tbsp for frying the eggs
60g smoked bacon lardons
2 eggs
salt and pepper

Wash the potatoes and put into a saucepan with salted water. Cover, bring to the boil and cook for 15 minutes until almost cooked through.

Drain the potatoes and rinse under a cold running tap. Peel the potatoes while still hot and put into a bowl. Leave to cool for 1 hour.

Once cool, cut the potatoes into rough chunks. Melt the lard in a large heavy-bottomed frying pan, and fry the bacon lardons in it for 2 minutes.

Add the potato chunks and make sure they cover the entire base of the saucepan. Fry on a medium heat for 5 minutes. Shake the frying pan and fry for another 5 minutes. Repeat this twice more so the potatoes fry on all sides for 20 minutes in total. Season with salt and pepper before serving.

Just before the potatoes have finished frying, melt 1 tablespoon of lard in a frying pan and fry 2 eggs to your liking. Season with salt and pepper and serve each portion of potatoes topped with a fried egg.

TIPS

• It is best to buy a whole piece of vacuum-packed bacon, which you chop into lardons yourself. The bacon will be firmer than pre-diced lardons and will withstand the heat of the frying pan for longer.

• It's easy to badly burn your fingers peeling the hot potatoes – my friend Laura gave me a great tip which she learnt in culinary school: crunch up a piece of foil and use it to hold the hot potato.

• If you have any leftover *gebootschte* potatoes, you can reheat them the next day in a frying pan with a bit of lard – they'll be even crispier and tastier then!

Judd mat Gaardebounen is as Luxembourgish as it gets. A hearty dish of smoked pork collar with broad beans in a creamy sauce. In my first book, I created a *Judd mat Gaardebounen pie* to give this traditional dish a British spin. I have been searching for innovative ways to further transform this staple ever since. My favourite so far comes with an Italian twist: cannelloni stuffed with a minced *Judd mat Gaardebounen* filling and snuggled in a creamy white wine béchamel. My little nod to the vast Italian community in Luxembourg...

JUDD MAT GAARDEBOUNEN CANNELLONI

❋ Serves 8 • Prep 1h30' • Oven 30' • A little effort ❋

For the Cannelloni:
1 onion
1 tbsp sunflower oil
400g frozen broad beans
450g cooked smoked pork collar (Judd)
½ flat bunch of parsley, chopped
4 tsp summer savoury (Bounekräitchen)
500g fresh lasagne sheets
150g cheese, grated

For the Béchamel:
90g butter
90g flour
750ml milk
200ml white wine
350ml cream
1 ½ tsp salt
pepper

Peel and chop the onion. Heat the sunflower oil in a frying pan and fry the onions for 4 minutes until soft.

Bring a saucepan with salted water to the boil and cook the broad beans for 5 minutes until soft. Drain and put into a blender without mixing yet. Cut the smoked pork collar into small chunks and add to the blender with the cooked onions, parsley and summer savoury and whizz into a chunky paste.

For the béchamel sauce, melt the butter in a saucepan, add the flour and fry on a medium heat for a couple of minutes until golden and fragrant. Gradually add the milk, whisking between each addition and leaving it to cook for a minute or so, so that it thickens and you get a smooth sauce. Then gradually add the white wine in the same way followed by the cream. Season with salt and pepper. Take off the heat, cover the saucepan with a lid and set aside.

Fill a saucepan with boiling salted water and, using tongs, briefly dip the lasagne sheets into the hot water, one at a time. Remove each lasagne sheet after a couple of seconds, so they soften only a little. Transfer to a colander and set aside.

Preheat the oven to 180°C fan.

Cover the bottom of a greased ceramic ovenproof dish with a layer of béchamel. Cut 1 lasagne sheet crosswise in 4 so that you end up with 4 small cannelloni sheets. If the sheets stick together, separate them by dipping them in a bowl with cold water.

Put 1 tablespoon of the filling along the base of 1 cannelloni sheet and roll up. Place the cannelloni on top of the béchamel, seam side down. Repeat until the dish is full.

Top the cannelloni with a layer of béchamel, then, place another layer of cannelloni on top, cover with béchamel and grated cheese.

Bake in the preheated oven for 30 minutes until the cheese is golden and the béchamel is bubbling.

Pastachutta is basically the same dish that Italian restaurants serve as *Bolognese*, but somehow the version people cook at home has become known as *Pastachutta* in Luxembourg.
I have countless memories eating huge bowls of *Pastachutta* at my grandma's; it was my favourite dish at hers. So, when researching this recipe I asked my grandma for the secret to her unforgettable *Pastachutta*. To which she just shrugged and said 'I always threw everything into a big pot, let it cook and in the end I mixed the sauce with the spaghetti before plating up.' So that's what I did... I hope you enjoy my version of *Pastachutta*!

PASTACHUTTA

❋ Serves 6-8 • Prep 1h30' • Easy ❋

1 onion
1 red chilli
2 carrots
1 small fennel bulb
3 rosemary sprigs
2 garlic cloves
1 tbsp olive oil
1 tbsp fennel seeds
750g mixed beef and
   pork mince
300ml red wine
1 can chopped
   tomatoes (400g)
500ml passata
1 tbsp tomato
   concentrate
½ tsp dried thyme
2 bay leaves
2 tsp Worcestershire
   sauce
salt and pepper

800g-1kg dried
   spaghetti
a knob of butter
Parmesan, to serve

Start by preparing your vegetables. Peel and finely chop the onion. Destem the chilli, slice open lengthwise, remove the seeds and finely chop. Peel the carrots and cut into little dice. Trim the fennel bulb, remove the stem and cut into little dice. Pick the rosemary leaves and finely chop. Peel and crush the garlic cloves.

Heat the olive oil in a large heavy-bottomed saucepan and fry the onion and chilli until soft, for about 4 minutes. Add the fennel seeds and the garlic and fry for another minute.

Raise the temperature to high, add the mince and fry until the meat has browned. Break up the meat, so you end up with a fine mince. Add the carrots and the fennel and fry for another couple of minutes.

Add the red wine, chopped tomatoes, passata, tomato concentrate, chopped rosemary, dried thyme and bay leaves and season generously with salt and pepper.

Cover and leave to simmer on a medium heat for 40 minutes, stirring from time to time.

After 40 minutes remove the lid and cook for another 10 minutes so the sauce thickens. Season with Worcestershire sauce and some more salt if necessary.

Cook the spaghetti according to packet instructions. Drain and add a knob of butter. Pour the sauce over the spaghetti and mix so the pasta is coated in sauce.

Plate up and sprinkle each portion with freshly grated parmesan.

 TIP I always make a big batch of Pastachutta sauce and freeze a few portions as a stand-by dinner saver.

Kniddelen are a true Luxembourg classic. These humble boiled dumplings are traditionally eaten with bacon lardons and a side of apple compote. I have had many vegetarian friends ask me for a meat-free alternative, so I have come up with this completely offbeat suggestion: *Kniddelen* in a creamy broccoli sauce sprinkled with smoked almonds. You could of course replace the almonds with fried bacon lardons if you want to please your meat-eating friends.

CREAMY BROCCOLI KNIDDELEN

Serves 6 • Prep 45' • Easy • Vegetarian

For the Kniddelen:
500g flour
200g quark
  (40% fat content)
4 eggs
250ml milk
½ tsp salt
pepper

1 broccoli
1 onion
2 garlic cloves
20g butter
300ml cream
50ml white wine
80g Parmesan, grated
salt and pepper

100g smoked almonds,
  to serve

Put all the Kniddelen ingredients into a large bowl and mix with an electric whisk until you get a smooth batter. Season with salt and pepper.

Fill a large saucepan with boiling water and add a generous pinch of salt. Dip a teaspoon into a bowl of cold water, then grab a portion of batter with the teaspoon, and dip it into the boiling water so the dumpling slides off into the saucepan and sinks to the bottom. Repeat until the bottom of the saucepan is covered with dumplings. Keep boiling until the dumplings float to the surface – then leave them to cook for another 2 minutes. Remove the dumplings from the water with a slotted spoon and put into a bowl, which you cover with a lid between additions to keep the Kniddelen warm. Repeat this process until all the batter is used up, cover and set aside.

Wash the broccoli and cut into small florets, cut the stem into 1cm wide sticks. Cook the broccoli in boiling salted water for 5 minutes. Drain and put into a blender.

While the broccoli is cooking, peel and finely chop the onion. Peel and crush the garlic cloves.

Heat the butter in a frying pan and fry the onions for 4 minutes until soft. Add the garlic to the onions, fry for another minute. Add to the blender.

Add the cream and the white wine to the blender and pulse into a puree. Put the broccoli puree into a large saucepan, add the cheese and reheat. Cook for a couple of minutes, season with salt and pepper, then add the Kniddelen and cook for a further 5 minutes until everything is heated through.

Chop the smoked almonds and sprinkle each portion of Kniddelen with some almonds.

I'm secretly looking forward to Brussels sprouts season all year long, as these little gems are one of my favourite brassica vegetables. I know many people who cringe at the mere thought of Brussels sprouts, but I've managed to convert quite a few ardent sprout haters by roasting the sprouts in the oven. Prepared that way, they retain a bit of a crunch and the outer leaves become crispy and slightly smoky. To amp up the smokiness of this dish, I'm sprinkling the sprouts with Scamorza – an Italian smoked cheese that works wonderfully in this comforting winter dish.

SMOKY BRUSSELS SPROUTS SPÄTZLE

❦ Serves 2 • Prep 50' • Easy ❦

300g Brussels sprouts, trimmed
2 tbsp olive oil
a pinch of dried chilli flakes
salt and pepper

For the pesto:
15g pine nuts
1 bunch of basil
½ garlic clove
20g Parmesan or Italian hard cheese
40ml olive oil
a pinch of salt

50g smoked Scamorza
20g butter
500g fresh Spätzle

Preheat the oven to 200°C fan.

Finely slice the Brussels sprouts – this is best done using a food processor equipped with a slicing blade or a mandolin.

Put the sprouts into a baking dish and drizzle with the olive oil, sprinkle with chilli flakes and a bit of salt and pepper. Bake for approximately 15 minutes, stirring from time to time until the sprouts are al dente and charred in places – the browned leaves will add some extra taste and texture.

While the sprouts are in the oven, prepare the pesto: Put all the ingredients into a blender and blitz into a slightly chunky pesto.

Cut the Scamorza into small dice and set aside.

Heat a frying pan and melt the butter. Add the Spätzle and fry for 5 to 10 minutes until heated through and crispy.

Remove the sprouts from the oven and stir through the pesto.

Divide the Spätzle between 2 plates, top with pesto sprouts and sprinkle with Scamorza cubes.

TIP — If you prefer this dish a bit less smoky, you can replace the Scamorza with mozzarella.

You may have noticed that spelt flour pasta shapes are becoming ever more popular and readily available in Luxembourg's supermarkets. Spelt is an ancient grain that is mostly grown in the north of the country, in the Upper Sûre Nature Reserve. You can buy local spelt flour, spelt flakes (an alternative to oats) and even spelt schnapps! I love using spelt pasta instead of regular pasta from time to time, and I think it works perfectly in this recipe. The lentils provide plenty of protein and you are guaranteed to leave the table with a full and happy belly.

LENTIL SPELT PASTA

❀ Serves 4 • Prep 45' • Easy • Vegetarian ❀

1 onion
1 garlic clove
200g green lentils
1 tbsp sunflower oil
250ml vegetable stock
400ml cream
¼ tsp salt
2 tsp summer savoury
  (Bounekräitchen)
3 tbsp sour cream
400g spelt pasta
pepper

grated cheese, to serve

Peel and finely chop the onion. Peel and crush the garlic clove. Rinse the lentils under a running tap.

Heat the sunflower oil in a saucepan and fry the onion for 4 minutes until soft. Add the garlic and fry for another minute. Add the lentils and fry for another minute.

Add the vegetable stock and 250ml of the cream, the salt and the summer savoury. Cover, bring to the boil and simmer for 30 minutes until the lentils are al dente.

Uncover and add the remaining 150ml cream and the sour cream, season with salt and pepper. Bring to the boil, take off the hob and cover.

Cook the spelt pasta according to package instructions until al dente. Drain and mix with the lentils.

Distribute the lentil pasta between 4 bowls and serve with a generous portion of cheese.

Yes, you could say this is a bastardized version of our beloved *Rieslingspaschtéit*. With curry powder. And mango chutney. And with *gasp*, coriander, too! It sounds completely wacky, but trust me, these bold flavours and *Rieslingspaschtéit* are a match made in heaven! I opted for a pie shape for these *Paschtéiten*, but you could just as well give them their traditional log shape (page 151).

CURRY RIESLINGSPASCHTÉIT

❧ Makes 24 • Prep 2h30' • Marinating overnight • Worth the effort ❧

For the dough:
600g flour
300g butter
15g salt
70ml lukewarm water
1 egg

For the filling:
200g veal shouler
600g minced veal
50ml Riesling or
   Elbling
2 tbsp mango chutney
2 ½ tsp curry powder
½ tsp cumin seeds
15g salt
1 shallot
1 bunch of coriander
1 egg

2 egg yolks, beaten
1 tbsp milk

On the first day, start by preparing the dough: Mix the flour and butter with an electric whisk. Dilute the salt in the lukewarm water and add to the flour mix with the egg. Beat to a smooth dough. Shape the dough into 2 discs, wrap in cling film and refrigerate overnight.

Cut the veal shoulder into cubes and put into a large container. Add the minced veal, white wine, mango chutney, curry powder, cumin seeds and salt. Mix well, cover and refrigerate overnight.

The next day, take the chilled dough of the fridge 1 hour before you intend to roll it out.

Peel and finely chop the shallot. Finely chop the coriander and add to the marinated meat with the chopped shallot and the egg. Mix well.

Make the egg wash by mixing the beaten egg yolks with 1 tablespoon of milk in a jar.

Grease the holes of a muffin tin and line the bottom of each hole with baking paper – this will make it easier to remove the Rieslingspaschtéiten after baking.

Preheat the oven to 160°C fan.

Unwrap the dough disks and place onto a lightly floured work surface. Roll out to 3mm thick.

Cut out 24 pastry discs large enough to line the inside of the muffin holes. Line each hole with a disc, pushing each disc in with your fingers so that it sticks to the bottom and sides.

Stuff each pie case with the meat filling.

Unroll the remaining dough and cut out 24 discs of approximately 8 cm to make the lids, cutting out a hole in the centre with an apple corer.

Brush the edges of the filled cases with the egg wash, then put the pastry lids on top. Press the edges with your fingers or with a fork to make sure they are firmly sealed. Brush the lids with the egg wash.

For the jelly:

2 sachets instant meat jelly (*Sülze*) for 2.5dl each

250ml water

250ml Riesling or Elbling

2 tbsp mango chutney

Bake the Rieslingspaschtéiten in the preheated oven for 45 minutes.

Just before they have finished baking, prepare the white wine jelly. Pour the instant meat jelly powder into a saucepan and add 250ml of boiling water, the wine and the mango chutney. Bring to the boil and stir until the jelly powder has completely dissolved. Pour the liquid into a jug.

Place the muffin tin with the Rieslingspaschtéiten on a wire rack. If there is anything clogging the little holes in the centre of the pastry lids, unclog them using a small spoon and clear the hole so that you can see the cooked meat inside. Leave to cool for 15 minutes.

After 15 minutes, pour some white wine jelly into the holes, all the way to the top. The pastries will gradually soak up the jelly, so let them rest for a few minutes and pour some more jelly into each hole once it has cleared up again. You may want to gently tilt the pastries from one side to the other, to ensure that the jelly really gets into all the cavities inside. Repeat this process until the pastries absorb no more liquid and the holes are completely filled with jelly.

Leave the pastries to cool completely for a few hours so that the jelly sets and take them out of the muffin tin once cold. Wrap in foil and store in the fridge.

The Rieslingspaschtéiten will keep in the fridge for over 1 week.

TRADITIONAL RIESLINGSPASCHTÉIT

10g white peppercorns

10g black peppercorns

5g marjoram

8g thyme

8g basil

8g nutmeg

8g mace

10g bay leaves

10g cloves

8g powdered ginger

10g mild paprika powder

5g spicy paprika powder

100g salt

For the traditional Rieslingspaschtéit, replace the mango chutney, curry powder and cumin seeds from the recipe page 146 with this spice mix.

Grind all the spices individually into a fine powder. You will need an electric spice or coffee grinder for this to work properly. Combine all the ground spices in a bowl, then take 10g of the ground spice mix and mix it with 100g salt in a separate jar.

Put the 800g of meat into a large container. Add 15g of the spiced salt and the white wine. Mix well, cover and refrigerate overnight.

Continue with the recipe, replacing the coriander with parsley and omitting the mango chutney from the jelly.

 TIP You will have a lot of leftover spice mix. Mix it with salt (at a 1:10 ratio) and fill into little jars as gifts.

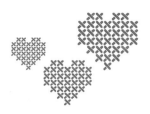

HOW TO CREATE THE TRADITIONAL LOG SHAPE

❧ For 8 Paschtéiten with the recipe page 146 ❧

Unwrap one dough disc and place onto a lightly floured work surface. Roll out into a square 3mm thick .

Put a heap of meat filling approximately 12cm long and 5 cm high in the centre of the square, leaving a generous border of approximately 10cm. Cut out a rectangle around the filling - the border needs to be wide enough so the long sides overlap by approximately 1 cm when you fold them over the meat filling.

Fold the long pastry sides over the meat filling, sealing the edges with some egg wash and gently patting the dough together.

Flatten the two shorter dough slabs to 3mm thick using a rolling pin. Cut off the excess dough so that you're left with 2 flattened side slabs of approximately 5cm. Brush each one with some egg wash and fold in over the sealed pasty. Gently pat the dough down so that it is nicely sealed – it is essential that the pastry is sealed so the jelly stays inside after baking and does not leak.

Turn over the pastry so the seams are on the bottom. Using an apple corer, cut out a small hole in the centre of the pastry so the meat is exposed.

Roll out a small piece of leftover dough to 3mm thick and cut out a wave-shaped circle with a cookie-cutter. Cut a hole into the middle of the circle with the apple corer.

Brush the pastry with egg wash, then stick the wave-shaped circle onto the pastry so both holes overlap. Brush the wave-shaped circle with egg wash. Use a fork to lightly scratch a cross pattern into the egg wash on both sides of the pastry circle – this will give the Rieslingspaschtéit its trademark look.

Place the Rieslingspaschtéiten on a baking tray lined with baking paper and bake at 160°C fan for 50 minutes.

"Can you guess my all-time favourite dish in the world?", my photographer Véronique Kolber asked on one of our shoots for this book. I shrugged. "I'll give you a clue, it's from Luxembourg...", she continued. I shrugged again. *Bouchée à la reine? Judd mat Gaardebounen?*
"No, it's boiled beef with cold egg sauce!" My jaw dropped! I had almost forgotten this Sunday lunch staple, which we often had at my grandma's when I was little. I didn't realize other people knew this dish, too! So, there was no way around it: I had to include beef with egg sauce in this book!

BEEF WITH EGG SAUCE

Serves 4 • Prep 20' • Cooking 3h • Easy

2 x 600g chuck (paleron)
1 onion
1 carrot
1 small leek
1 bay leaf
3 peppercorns
1 tbsp coarse salt

For the egg sauce:
8 eggs
250ml cream
5 tbsp mustard
a dash of white wine vinegar
salt and pepper

Tie the meat in 3 places with butcher's string so it holds its shape while boiling.

Wash the unpeeled onion, cut in half and place cut-side down into a large heavy-bottomed saucepan. Put over a high heat and burn the onion on the cut side for a few minutes until slightly charred.

Fill the saucepan with boiling water and add the carrot, leek, bay leaf, peppercorns, salt and meat to the onions. Reduce the heat, cover and simmer for 3 hours, until the meat is tender. You may have to top up the water from time to time to keep the brisket covered.

Meanwhile, prepare the sauce. Put the eggs into a saucepan with boiling water and boil for 10 minutes. Drain and leave to cool for a bit. Peel and quarter the eggs, then mash with a fork.

Put the mashed eggs into a bowl, add the cream and mustard and mix to combine. Season to taste with a dash of white wine vinegar and salt and pepper.

Once the meat is tender, cut into slices and serve with the cold egg sauce and a side of boiled potatoes.

TIP

Strain the cooking liquid, fill into jars and freeze – it makes a really good light stock.

Toad in the hole is one of those British oddities that no one outside of the UK seems to have ever come across... The dish consists of sausages snuggled in an oven-baked pancake batter drizzled with gravy. It is not the most photogenic or elegant dish, but many would say that toad in the hole is a staple of British childhood. Most Luxembourgers would say the same about *Wäinzoossiss*, a sausage made with wine and traditionally served with a creamy mustard sauce. I decided it was time for these dishes to get acquainted and they seem to have hit it off: this Luxembourg/British hybrid totally rocks!

WÄINZOOSSISS TOAD IN THE HOLE

❤ Serves 4 • Prep 45' • Easy ❤

4 eggs
2 tbsp wholegrain mustard
170g flour
170ml milk
170ml lager beer
1/2 tsp salt
pepper
4 tbsp sunflower oil
8 Wäinzoossiss or sausages

For the mustard sauce:
1 shallot
25g butter
80ml white wine
200ml cream
2 tbsp wholegrain mustard
salt and pepper

Preheat the oven to 200°C fan.

Start by preparing the batter: beat the eggs and mustard together in a large bowl. Add the flour and beat into a smooth batter, gradually adding the milk and the beer. Season with the salt and some pepper. Set the batter aside to rest for 15 minutes.

Meanwhile, put 4 tablespoons of sunflower oil into a non-stick roasting tin. Place the sausages into the oil. Bake in the preheated oven for 10 minutes, turning them halfway through.

Once the sausages have baked for 10 minutes, take the roasting tin out of the oven, quickly pour in all the batter and put the tin back into the oven. Leave to bake for 25 minutes without opening the oven door.

While the toad in the hole is baking, prepare the mustard sauce. Peel and finely chop the shallot. Melt the butter in a saucepan and fry the shallot for 4 minutes until soft. Add the white wine and cook for 3 minutes.

Mix the cream with the mustard and add to the saucepan, simmer for another 3 minutes. Season with salt and pepper.

Serve the toad in the hole straight out of the oven, drizzle with some mustard sauce and serve with a green salad.

If there's one dish that screams winter comfort food it must be *choucroute*. *Sauerkraut* served with smoky meats and buttery potato purée – nothing could be better to warm the heart and spirit on a cold and rainy day. In Luxembourg, *choucroute* is often served with liver dumplings. I'm not very fond of those, so I've omitted them here. Instead, I've spiced up my *choucroute* with a bit of paprika powder and a sprinkle of caraway seeds to add an additional flavour dimension.

CHOUCROUTE

❦ Serves 4 • Prep 1h 30' • Easy ❦

1kg natural sauerkraut
1 onion
2 garlic cloves
2 apples
20g butter
200g smoked bacon lardons
¼ tsp chilli flakes
2 tsp paprika powder
1 tsp caraway seeds
6 juniper berries
2 cloves
2 bay leaves
250ml white wine
750ml chicken stock
400g uncooked smoked pork collar (Judd or Kassler)
16 'mixed mini apéro sausages'
mustard, to serve

Put the sauerkraut into a sieve and squeeze out any excess liquid. Set aside.

Peel and finely chop the onion. Peel and crush the garlic cloves. Peel and core the apples and cut into bite sized chunks.

Heat the butter in a large, heavy-bottomed saucepan with a lid and fry the lardons for 3 minutes. Add the chopped onion and fry for 4 minutes until the onions are soft. Add the crushed garlic, chilli flakes, paprika powder and caraway seeds and fry for another minute.

Add the sauerkraut, the chopped apples, juniper berries, cloves, bay leaves, white wine and chicken stock. Place the smoked pork collar on top of the sauerkraut, cover the saucepan and simmer for 50 minutes.

After 50 minutes, uncover the choucroute and stick the mini sausages into the sauerkraut so that they're completely covered. Simmer for another 10 minutes.

Take the smoked pork collar out of the saucepan and cut into 4 slices.

Arrange some sauerkraut, a slice of smoked pork collar and 4 sausages on each plate. Serve with a dollop of mustard and potato puree.

TIPS

• Some sauerkraut comes precooked in white wine. Since it's being cooked with wine and spices, you're looking for natural, unflavoured sauerkraut for this recipe.

• Mixed apéro sausages usually include *Mettwurscht*, *Frankfurter*, *Käsekrainer* and *Lëtzebuerger Grillwurscht*. If you can't get hold of these, you can buy some *Mettwurscht* and *Frankfurter* sausages instead.

• Any leftovers can be made into *Tierteg* fritters the next day. Just boil a few potatoes while cooking the choucroute and set them aside for the *Tierteg*. Mash them and keep in the fridge overnight. The next day, mix the mashed potatoes with an equal amount of leftover sauerkraut and some chopped meat. Shape into patties, dip them into a bit of flour and fry them in a generous amount of butter for a few minutes on each side until crispy and warmed through.

When we were little we would often eat roast chicken with apple sauce and chips. It was one of my favourite meals and still goes down a treat. This is the grown-up version. Roast chicken legs on a bed of cider-laced apples and served with Hasselback potatoes – baked potatoes that are thinly sliced to get a crispy outside.

CIDER CHICKEN
WITH HASSELBACK POTATOES

❀ Serves 2 • Prep 1h • Oven 50' • A little effort ❀

1 onion
2 tbsp olive oil
2 apples (Braeburn)
½ cinnamon stick
250ml cider
100ml chicken stock
1 garlic clove
4 sage leaves
2 chicken legs
1 tbsp cornflour
salt and pepper

Preheat the oven to 180°C fan.

Peel and slice the onion. Heat 1 tbsp olive oil in a frying pan and fry the onion slices for 4 minutes until soft. Put into a roasting tin and set aside.

Peel and core the apples and cut into bite-sized chunks. Put into the frying pan along with the cinnamon stick, ½ tsp salt, the cider and chicken stock. Bring to the boil, then add to the onions in the roasting tin.

Peel and slice the garlic clove. Slide your finger under the skin of a chicken leg to make a little pocket. Stuff each pocket with 2 sage leaves and a few slices of garlic. Season the chicken all over with salt and pepper.

Heat 1 tbsp olive oil in the frying pan and brown the chicken legs on all sides. Place the browned legs on top of the apples in the roasting tin. Cover the roasting tin with foil, put into the preheated oven and bake for 45 minutes.

After 30 minutes, remove the foil from the chicken so that the chicken skin can crisp up.

After 45 minutes, check that the chicken is cooked through (the juices need to run clear) – if not, roast a little longer. Put the chicken legs on a plate and cover with foil while you finish the sauce.

Pour the apples and the liquid left in the roasting tin into a frying pan. Bring to the boil. Dilute the cornflour in 2 tbsp of cold water and add to the boiling sauce. Stir until you get a thick sauce.

Serve the chicken with apple sauce and a side of cabbage and Hasselback potatoes.

HASSELBACK POTATOES

6 medium waxy
  potatoes
2 tbsp olive oil
25g butter, melted
2 garlic cloves
1 rosemary sprig
salt

Preheat the oven to 180°C fan.

Put the potatoes skin on into a saucepan filled with salted water, bring to the boil and cook for 6 minutes. Drain and leave to cool for a few minutes.

Place a potato onto a wooden spoon, then cut thin slices into the potato – the knife will hit the wooden spoon about two-thirds into the potato, preventing you from cutting all the way through.

Heat 2 tbsp of olive oil in a frying pan. Fry the potatoes for 10 minutes, turning them from time to time so they start to crisp up on the outside.

Pour 25g of melted butter into a roasting tin, add the potatoes and toss them in the butter until evenly coated. Lightly bash the garlic cloves and add them to the roasting tin with the rosemary and a generous sprinkle of salt. Bake in the preheated oven for 1 hour, turning the potatoes halfway through.

CIDER CABBAGE

¼ Savoy cabbage
1 small leek
25g butter
1 garlic clove
50ml cider
50ml cream
salt and pepper

Core the cabbage and slice the leaves. Cook in a saucepan with boiling salted water for 5 minutes. Drain and rinse with cold water to retain the vibrant green colour.

Trim the leek and finely slice. Heat the butter in a large frying pan and fry the leek for a few minutes until soft. Peel and crush the garlic clove, add to the leek and fry for another minute. Add the blanched cabbage and the cider and fry for a few minutes until most of the liquid has been absorbed. Add the cream, heat through and season with salt and pepper.

TIP

As you don't need much cabbage for this recipe, you could make *okonomiyaki* (page 102) with the leftover cabbage. Alternatively, I like to stir-fry strips of cabbage in a bit of oil with a dash of soy sauce and a sprinkling of fennel seeds and chilli flakes and serve them on a bowl of rice with a fried egg.

I first ate lemongrass pork on a market in Thailand – sticky, fragrant, succulent grilled meat with an unparalleled taste; totally addictive! I later found out it was actually a Vietnamese and not a Thai recipe, but, as they'd say in Southeast Asia, it's 'same same'. Since we eat a lot of barbecued pork cutlets in Luxembourg during the summer, usually in a paprika-based marinade, I thought I'd put forward this recipe as a refreshing alternative.

LEMONGRASS CÔTELETTES

❦ Serves 2 • Prep 20' • Marinating overnight • Easy ❦

2 x 250g côtelettes
  (pork chops)

For the marinade:
2 lemongrass sticks
½ shallot
1 garlic clove
10 black peppercorns
1 ½ tbsp brown sugar
1 ½ tsp ketjap manis or
  sweet soy sauce
1 ½ tbsp Thai fish sauce
1 tbsp sunflower oil
a pinch of chilli flakes

sriracha sauce, to serve

Starting a day ahead, trim the lemongrass sticks and remove the outer layer. Finely chop and put into a pestle and mortar, then pound into a paste.

Finely chop the shallot and add to the lemongrass in the pestle and mortar, pound into a paste. Peel and crush the garlic clove and add to the pestle and mortar. Add the peppercorns and crush.

Finally, add all the remaining marinade ingredients and pound into a smooth paste.

Put the côtelettes into a Ziploc bag, add the marinade and massage into the meat. Close the bag, pressing out as much air as you can. Refrigerate overnight.

The next day, heat the barbecue and wait for the flames to die down. Take the côtelettes out of the bag and pour the leftover marinade into a bowl.

Place the côtelettes onto the grill and grill for about 8 minutes, turning them over halfway through and brushing them with the marinade from time to time.

Serve with sriracha sauce as a spicy dip.

TIPS

• There are various *côtelette* cuts available in Luxembourg: *côte collet de porc* is a bit marbled, with fat running through it. If you prefer a leaner cut, go for *côte première de porc*.

• You can blitz all the marinade ingredients in a food processor, but the paste will be less fine.

• I like to accompany these *côtelettes* with my winter slaw (page 78).

I have a confession to make: I am not really a big meat eater. Yes, I do cook with meat but I do not often cook any big cut of meat. So for this recipe I asked my friend Ben, Luxembourg's BBQ master, for a hand. He showed me how to prepare a *côte à l'os* by pre-grilling it and finishing it off in the oven – leaving plenty of time to rustle together some tasty sides to go with it. The result is a really tender and juicy piece of meat, totally delicious!

CÔTE À L'OS
WITH HORSERADISH BUTTER

❦ Serves 4 • Prep 45' • Easy ❦

1kg rib eye on the bone
500g fine French
  beans
8 smoked bacon
  rashers
1 tbsp olive oil
salt and pepper

horseradish butter,
  to serve
potato gratin, to serve

Preheat the oven to 120°C fan.

Heat a griddle pan to high and grill the rib eye for 5 minutes on one side. After 5 minutes, flip over and grill for 2 minutes on the other side. Then flip the meat over and grill both sides again for another 2 minutes. Put into a roasting tin and leave to rest for 10 minutes.

After 10 minutes, pop the meat it into the oven and roast for 20 minutes.

Meanwhile, prepare the beans. Trim the beans and cook in a saucepan with salted water for a few minutes until cooked through. Drain in a colander and rinse with cold water to seal in the green colour.

Lay out a strip of bacon, place a handful of beans on one end and roll up tightly. Repeat with the remaining beans so you get 8 parcels.

Heat a tablespoon of olive oil in a frying pan and fry the bacon-wrapped beans on all sides, season with pepper.

After 20 minutes, take the meat out of the oven and cut into slices, arrange on 4 plates, season with salt and pepper and top the meat with horseradish butter.

Serve each portion with 2 bacon-wrapped bean parcels and patato gratin.

POTATO GRATIN

600g waxy potatoes
1 garlic clove
30g butter
125ml milk
125ml cream
1 egg
50g cheese, grated
a pinch of nutmeg
salt and pepper

Preheat the oven to 180°C fan.

Peel the potatoes and slice as thinly as possible in a food processor.

Rub a baking dish with a peeled garlic clove, allowing it to absorb some flavour, then butter the dish.

Distribute the potato slices in the baking dish.

Melt the butter; mix with the milk, cream, egg and cheese. Add a pinch of nutmeg and season with salt and pepper.

Pour the milk mix over the potatoes and bake for 50 minutes until cooked through.

HORSERADISH BUTTER

100g butter, soft
½ garlic clove
1 tsp fresh rosemary, chopped
2 tbsp horseradish cream
salt and pepper

Put the soft butter into a bowl and beat with a fork until creamy.

Crush the half garlic clove and add to the butter with the rosemary and horseradish cream. Season generously with salt and pepper – you want it to be quite salty. Put on a sheet of cling film, wrap into a log and refrigerate until needed.

TIP

The horseradish butter will keep in the fridge for 2 weeks. You can spread it on toast, fry mushrooms in it or use it to flavour cooked peas or potatoes.

I made a huge batch of this chilli with the scouts at the UDACA *Scoutskiermes* in Lorentzweiler and it went down a treat. For me, proper chilli con carne needs a smoky dimension, which is very hard to achieve if you don't have access to chipotle chillies (a smoky, Mexican chilli variety). Don't despair though - by using a combination of smoked paprika powder and smoky *Mettwurscht* sausage from Luxembourg, I managed to really amp up the smokiness! Believe me, it is downright yummy. Serve it topped with sour cream and coriander to add some freshness to the dish, and with the first bite you will be in chilli heaven!

CHILLI CON METTWURSCHT

Serves 6 • Prep 1h30' • Easy

1 onion
2 garlic cloves
3 peppers
2 tbsp sunflower oil
550g mixed pork + beef mince
2 tsp paprika powder
2 tsp smoked paprika powder
½ tsp dried chilli flakes
2 tsp cumin powder
2 tsp marjoram
1 tsp dried thyme
2 tbsp tomato paste
1 tsp sugar
800g tinned chopped tomatoes
330ml Wëllen Ourdaller or dark beer
1 tbsp Worcestershire sauce
3 Mettwurscht sausages
500g tinned black beans, drained

To serve:
sour cream
coriander
pitta bread

Peel and finely chop the onion. Peel and crush the garlic cloves.

Wash the peppers, core, remove the seeds and cut into bite sized pieces.

Heat the sunflower oil in a large, heavy-bottomed saucepan. Fry the onion for 4 minutes until soft, then add the crushed garlic and fry for another minute.

Add the peppers and a pinch of salt and fry for another 5 minutes.

Add the mince and fry until the meat has lost its pink colour.

Add all the spices and fry for another couple of minutes.

Add the tomato paste, sugar, tinned chopped tomatoes, beer and Worcestershire sauce and season with another generous pinch of salt.

Cover and bring to the boil, reduce the heat and simmer for 45 minutes, stirring from time to time.

Meanwhile, cut the Mettwurscht sausages lengthwise in half and fry in a pan for 2 minutes on each side.

Put onto a chopping board and leave to cool. When cool enough to handle, halve each slice lengthwise and chop into little dice. Set aside.

After 45 minutes, add the Mettwurscht dice and the black beans to the saucepan and give it a stir. Cover and simmer for another 5 minutes. Season with more salt if needed.

Serve each portion of chilli topped with a dollop of sour cream, coriander and a side of pitta bread.

TIP

If you can't find smoked paprika powder you can use regular paprika powder.

SCOUTS RESTo

Kees

INFIRMERIE
& TOILETTEN

Kaffisst☕ff

When I lived in the UK, I often had to explain that a person from Luxembourg is called a Luxembourger. This was usually met with giggles, probably because I pretended to bite into a burger whenever I said it. That imaginary burger became the LuxemBurger for this book. I played around with various ideas and here is the one that won it: a juicy meat patty flavoured with *Mettwurscht*, a smoky sausage from Luxembourg. I also threw some *Kachkéis* into the mix and topped the whole thing with *sauerkraut* to add some tang. A patriotic burger that's best served with *Gromperekichelcher* nuggets, obviously! I suggest you make the burger buns yourself – it's definitely worth the effort as they taste amazing! No one will raise an eyebrow though if you decide to use shop-bought buns instead.

LUXEMBURGER

🌸 Serves 6 • Prep 20' • Easy 🌸

For the patties:

3 Mettwurscht
  sausages
350g mixed pork and
  beef mince
1 egg
3 tbsp breadcrumbs
2 tbsp sunflower oil

6 burger buns
1 small jar of sauerkraut
  cooked in wine
Mustard
1 pot of Kachkéis
Lamb's lettuce

Cut the Mettwurscht sausages lengthwise in half and scrape out the filling with a spoon. Discard the skin and put the sausage meat into a bowl with the mince, egg and breadcrumbs. Mix to combine and form into 6 patties.

Heat 2 tablespoons of sunflower oil in a frying pan and fry the patties for approximately 3 minutes on one side. Flip them over, cover the pan with a lid and fry for another 7 minutes, turning them from time to time, until cooked through. Put on a plate and cover with foil.

Slice the burger buns in half and toast them briefly cut-side down in the pan used to fry the patties.

Heat up the sauerkraut in the microwave.

Spread a dollop of mustard over the base of each burger bun, top with some Kachkéis and some lamb's lettuce. Place the burger patty on top, spread a generous spoonful of warm sauerkraut over the patty and top with the bun lids.

Serve with Gromperkichelcher nuggets (page 19) on the side.

BRIOCHE BURGER BUNS

❀ Makes 6 • Prep 20' • Rising 1h 20' • Oven 15' • A little effort ❀

450g strong white
  bread flour + extra for
  dusting (see tip
  below)
8g salt
33g sugar
15g fresh yeast
250ml water, lukewarm
75g butter, soft
1 egg, to glaze

In a bowl mix the flour, salt and sugar.

Crumble the yeast into a jar and mix with the lukewarm water until diluted.

Add the yeasty water to the flour and knead for approximately 5 minutes in a stand alone mixer fitted with a dough hook attachment or with your hands. Shape the dough into a ball, dust with flour, and cover the bowl with a damp tea towel. Leave to rise for 10 minutes.

After the 10 minutes, cut the butter into cubes and add to the dough. Mix until incorporated, then knead for another minute. The dough will be quite sticky. Cover the bowl with the damp tea towel and leave to rise for another 10 minutes.

After the 10 minutes, divide the dough into 6 equal pieces, roll each piece in some flour and shape into a ball. Place the burger buns on a baking tray lined with baking paper, leaving enough space between them, as they will rise in the oven. Cover with the damp tea towel and leave to rise for 1 hour at room temperature.

After an hour, preheat the oven to 200°C fan.

Beat the egg and brush the tops of the buns with the beaten egg glaze.

Bake the buns in the preheated oven for 15 minutes. Put on a wire rack to cool.

TIPS

• Make sure you buy plain strong bread flour without added raising agent. If you can't find any, you can use regular flour (type 55), but the buns won't be as fluffy.

• The buns freeze very well and they're great as breakfast brioche with jam, so why not make a double portion to make sure you have leftovers?

In the UK, baked ham is a favourite on Christmas day; in the US, turkey's on the menu, but in Luxembourg there is no set Christmas dinner tradition. Some people serve roast beef, others opt for game and some of my friends even have *Raclette* on Christmas Eve! So, why not surprise your guests with a rustic pulled pork dinner this year?! Pulled pork is perfect for entertaining large groups, as you can prepare a big batch ahead and feed plenty of hungry mouths with it. A great way to use up any leftovers is to make fiery pulled pork tacos: simply stuff a generous amount of meat into a tortilla wrap with some crunchy iceberg salad and a dollop of sriracha mayonnaise (page 98).

PULLED PORK WITH BACON-WRAPPED PEARS

❋ Serves 8-10 • Prep 40' • Oven 9h • Takes some time ❋

For the pulled pork:
2.2kg boneless pork
   shoulder joint
150ml cider
50ml cider vinegar
80ml maple syrup
50ml soy sauce
3 tbsp oyster sauce
1 tbsp fennel seeds
1 tbsp cumin seeds
4 cinnamon sticks
2 star anise
1 ½ tsp black
   peppercorns, crushed
1 ½ tsp smoked paprika
3 garlic cloves, crushed
1 tsp chilli flakes
2 tsp salt

To serve:
Fresh coriander,
   chopped
lingonberries, in syrup

Preheat the oven to 130°C fan.

Heat a griddle pan and fry the pork on all sides for approximately 8 minutes. Set aside.

Put all the ingredients except the pork shoulder into a heavy-bottomed saucepan that's large enough to snugly fit the pork joint. Put on the hob and bring to a simmer.

Remove the saucepan from the hob and place the pork joint into the hot liquid. Close with a lid and cook in the oven for 1 hour, turning the meat halfway through.

After 1 hour, reduce the oven temperature to 110°C and cook for another 2 hours, turning the meat halfway through.

After 2 hours, reduce the temperature to 100°C fan and cook for another 6 hours, turning the meat every hour and a half, until the meat is really soft.

Once the meat is really soft, remove it from the casserole and, using two forks, shred into bite sized pieces. Put the shredded meat back into the saucepan and toss it so that it soaks up some of the juices.

Arrange a serving of pulled pork on each plate, sprinkle with coriander and add a spoonful of lingonberries and 2 bacon-wrapped pears.

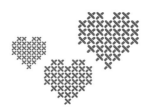

BACON-WRAPPED PEARS

1 tin of pears (820g)
8 bacon rashers
1 tbsp olive oil

Drain the pears and cut into 16 quarters.

Lay out the bacon rashers and halve lengthwise so you get 16 long strips. Wrap each strip around a pear quarter.

Heat the olive oil in a frying pan and fry the bacon-wrapped pears on both sides until the bacon is lightly browned.

Late autumn and early winter is game season in Luxembourg and you'll find many restaurants serving wild boar and venison dishes. I tend to associate game dishes with their delicious accompaniments. At home we would always eat them with a side of *Spätzle* and a pear stuffed with lingonberries. For this recipe I went a bit *off-piste*, replacing the *Spätzle* with traditional Luxembourg dumplings and sprinkling each serving with pomegranate seeds – the bright red rubies add a fresh zing to this comforting winter dish.

VENISON STEW WITH KNIDDELEN & POMEGRANATE

❋ Serves 6 • Prep 3h • Marinating overnight • A little effort ❋

For the stew:
1.2kg venison stew meat ('bîche', neck or shoulder)
4 shallots
4 garlic cloves
3 carrots
400ml red wine
2 tbsp brandy
2 tbsp olive oil
3 cloves
2 bouquet garni herb bags
3 bay leaves
8 thyme sprigs
1 tsp fennel seeds
100g smoked bacon lardons
40g butter
1 tbsp flour
1 tbsp dark chocolate
salt and pepper

seeds from ½ pomegranate
1 bunch of flat-leaf parsley, chopped

For the Kniddelen:
See page 136

Start by marinating the meat the night before: Cut the meat into 5 cm pieces and put into a large sealable container.

Peel and roughly chop the shallots. Peel the garlic cloves and the carrots and cut into slices. Add everything to the meat together with the wine, brandy, olive oil, cloves, bouquet garni herb bags, bay leaves, thyme sprigs, fennel seeds and some salt and pepper. Stir, cover and refrigerate overnight, stirring from time to time.

The next day, fry the bacon lardons in a large, heavy-bottomed saucepan until browned. Take out of the saucepan and set aside.

Remove the meat pieces from the marinating liquid and pat dry on kitchen paper. Add the butter to the saucepan used for the bacon and brown the meat in batches.

Once all the meat is browned, put it back into the saucepan together with the bacon lardons. Add the flour and stir, then add the marinating liquid including the aromatics.

Cover the saucepan and simmer over a medium heat for 2 ½ hours, stirring from time to time.

Once the stew has been cooking for 1 ½ hours, prepare the Kniddelen following the recipe on page 136.

Once the stew has been cooking for 2 ½ hours check that the meat is soft. Remove the bouquet garni, the thyme and bay leaves. Grate the chocolate and add to the stew; season with salt and pepper if needed.

Arrange a serving of Kniddelen on each plate, top with venison stew and finish off the dish with a sprinkling of pomegranate seeds and chopped parsley.

Trout is a fish native to Luxembourg's rivers, so you'll find trout on many local restaurant menus. My favourite way to eat it is pan-fried in plenty of butter and topped with almonds, which is the way my grandmother always cooked it for me and my sister when we were little. As a freshwater fish, trout has a really mild flavour, so I serve it on a bed of courgette slices here. Their subtle taste does not overpower the delicate flavour of the fish.

ALMOND BUTTER TROUT

❦ Serves 2 • Prep 40' • Quick & Easy ❦

2 small courgettes
1 shallot
1 garlic clove
85g butter
2 trout, scaled and
  gutted
3 tbsp flour
40g flaked almonds
lemon wedges,
  to serve
salt and pepper

Trim the courgettes and cut into thin slices. Peel and finely chop the shallot. Peel and crush the garlic.

Melt 25g of butter in a frying pan and fry the shallot for 4 minutes until soft. Add the garlic and fry for another minute.

Add the courgette slices and a pinch of salt and pepper and fry over a medium heat for 8 minutes until soft.

Meanwhile, rinse the trout under a cold running tap and pat dry on kitchen paper.

Put the flour on a plate and season with salt and pepper.

Melt 30g of butter in a large frying pan. Dip the trout into the seasoned flour so they are completely coated in flour, and place into the melted butter in the frying pan.

Fry over a medium heat for 4 minutes on each side, basting the trout with melted butter from time to time.

After 8 minutes, put the trout onto 2 serving plates.

Add the remaining 30g of butter and the almonds to the leftover butter in the frying pan. Melt over a high heat so the butter becomes frothy and smells nutty.

Pour over the trout and serve with the courgette slices and lemon wedges on the side.

This is a really impressive main course that's perfect for dinner parties. It's easy to prepare in advance and pop in the oven once your guests arrive.

SALMON EN CROUTE

❀ Serves 4 • Prep 40' • Fridge 15' • Oven 25' • Easy ❀

175g baby spinach leaves
50g garlic and herb soft cheese
lemon juice
500g salmon fillet, skinned
230g all-butter puff pastry
1 egg, beaten
salt and pepper

Wash the spinach. Bring a saucepan with salted water to the boil and blanch the spinach leaves for 1 minute. Drain and rinse with cold water so the spinach keeps its vibrant green colour. Squeeze out as much liquid as you can and put the spinach into a blender.

Add the garlic and herb soft cheese to the blender and blend into a paste. Season with a bit of lemon juice and salt and pepper.

Cut the salmon fillet in half so you end up with two equal-sized pieces. Season with salt and pepper.

Unroll the puff pastry and place one salmon piece into the centre of the dough. Spread the spinach paste over the salmon and top with the second piece of salmon.

Cut a 1 cm border into the dough around the salmon and brush the border with beaten egg.

Cut little pastry discs from the leftover pastry using a cookie cutter or shot glass, kneading together and re-rolling the pastry to use it all up. Starting on the 1 cm border, place the discs on the sides and on top of the salmon, overlapping them so that they eventually cover the entire surface and look like scales. Fold in the border at the bottom to create a rim.

Lift the salmon pastry into a metal baking dish lined with baking paper and refrigerate for 15 minutes.

Meanwhile, preheat the oven to 200°C fan.

After 15 minutes, take the salmon pastry out of the fridge and brush the pastry surface with beaten egg. Bake in the preheated oven for 25 minutes.

Serve with a green salad and potato purée.

TIP

You can prepare the salmon pastry a few hours ahead and keep it in the fridge until ready to bake.

I love pairing the aromatic flavour of tarragon with fish, so these sole and salmon roulades are bursting with its herby goodness. They are served with a sauce made with the delectable juices the fish releases in the oven. A fancy fish dish for a special occasion!

SOLE & SALMON ROULADES

❄ Serves 4 • Prep 1h • A little effort ❄

320g salmon fillet, skinned
8 sole fillets, skinned
1 bunch tarragon
1 bay leaf
5 peppercorns
75ml white wine
salt and pepper

For the sides:
500g baby spinach leaves
1 onion
2 garlic cloves
30g butter
4 tbsp cream cheese (or 80ml cream)

For the sauce:
30g butter
2 tbsp flour
160ml white wine
240ml cream

Preheat the oven to 180°C fan.

Cut the salmon into eight long slices.

Lay out the sole fillets, season with salt and pepper, then top with a few tarragon leaves.

Place a salmon slice at the end of each sole fillet and roll them up, securing them with a toothpick.

Grease an ovenproof dish that snugly fits the roulades. Put the roulades into the dish, add the bay leaf and peppercorns and pour over the white wine. Cover the dish with foil and bake the fish for 20 minutes.

Meanwhile, prepare the spinach. Blanch the leaves in a large saucepan with boiling salted water for 1 minute. Drain in a sieve, squeezing out most of the liquid, and set aside.

Peel and finely chop the onion. Peel and crush the garlic cloves. Melt the butter in a large frying pan and fry the onion for 4 minutes until soft. Add the garlic and fry for another minute. Add the drained spinach and the cream cheese and heat through. Season with salt and pepper, cover and set aside until ready to serve.

Once the fish is done, switch off the oven and strain the liquid from the ovenproof dish into a bowl. Put the roulades back into the warm oven while making the sauce.

For the sauce, melt the butter in a saucepan, add the flour and fry for a couple of minutes. Add the white wine and leave it to cook for a minute or so, so that it thickens. Gradually add the fish juices and the cream in the same way. Once you have a smooth sauce season with salt and pepper.

Take the fish out of the oven. If there are more juices in the ovenproof dish add them to the sauce.

Put 2 roulades onto each plate and serve with sauce, spinach and rice.

We might be a landlocked country, but we love mussels just as much as our Belgian neighbours do. The classic *Moulen à la crème mat Fritten* (Mussels in a cream sauce with chips) is an absolute must during mussel season: the mussels are steamed in a white wine broth and finished off with a generous glug of cream. I'm putting forward a more exotic way to prepare mussels, in a fragrant Thai broth with a dash of coconut cream.

THAI-STYLE MUSSELS

❋ Serves 2 • Prep 45' • Easy ❋

1kg mussels
1 shallot
1 red chilli
10g ginger
1 lemongrass
300ml chicken stock
2 kaffir lime leaves
100ml coconut cream
coriander, to serve

Start by cleaning the mussels. Put the mussels into a colander and rinse with cold water. Check each mussel individually, discarding any mussels with cracked shells and tapping on those that are open – in a live mussel, this will trigger a reaction to close its shell. If the mussel doesn't close, it has died and should be discarded. If any of the mussels have beards sticking out of the shell, debeard them by pulling off the hairs. Rinse the cleaned mussels again and set aside.

Peel and slice the shallot. Trim the chilli (and deseed if you don't want the dish to be too spicy) and finely slice. Peel the ginger and cut into small cubes. Bash the lemongrass stalk with a pestle or a rolling pin.

Heat the chicken stock in a large saucepan and add the shallot, chilli, ginger, lemongrass and lime leaves. Bring to the boil, cover and cook for 8 minutes to infuse the flavours.

Remove the lid and check that the liquid is at a roaring boil. Add the mussels to the saucepan and cover with the lid immediately. Cook with the lid on for 3 minutes, shaking the saucepan once or twice during cooking, with the lid still on.

After 3 minutes, remove the lid and check the mussels. Nearly all the mussels should be open by now. If not, cover and cook an additional 1 to 2 minutes. Mussels that haven't opened should be discarded.

Pour the coconut cream over the mussels, and serve with coriander and crusty bread or rice.

TIPS

• Kaffir lime leaves are fragrant leaves widely used in Thai cuisine, similar to how bay leaves are used in French cuisine. They taste very fresh, zingy and aromatic and are the key ingredient in many Southeast Asian dishes. You can find bags of frozen kaffir lime leaves in the freezer section of most Asian supermarkets. I always keep a bag in my freezer, it's a handy way to always have some at hand to satisfy your Thai cravings.

• Unfortunately reheating unshelled mussels is not advised, so if you have any leftover mussels, take them out of their shells and use them in a salad or serve them cold with some mayonnaise.

• If you have any leftover cooking liquid, it makes for a lovely soup – you can add some bean sprouts and rice noodles to bulk it up.

Over the past few years, a slight gin craze has swept over Luxembourg's eating and drinking establishments. Lots of bars have started putting a large variety of well-known and obscure gins on their drinks menus that they pair with different tonics and aromatics. You can even find Luxembourg gins on bar shelves now. They are very good and definitely worth a try! No need to use any fancy gin for this recipe though, as the strawberries will infuse the gin and give it a sweet , fruity note – a refreshing springtime G&T. Prost!

STRAWBERRY G&T

Makes 6 • Prep 10' • Infusing 30' • Easy

300ml gin
½ tsp black
  peppercorns
8 strawberries
4 sprigs of mint
1.2l tonic water
1 lime

Pour the gin into a jug.

Put the peppercorns into a teabag and add to the gin.

Trim the strawberries, cut into chunks and add to the gin together with the sprigs of mint. Leave to infuse for at least 30 minutes.

Remove the teabag with the peppercorns from the gin.

Pour 50ml gin into 6 glasses and distribute the strawberries evenly between the glasses.

Top up each glass with 200ml tonic water and add a bit of lime juice to taste.

Kir au vin blanc is a classic in my house. In the summer I like to pour my kir into popsicle moulds and freeze it. Your aperitif could not be more refreshing!

KIR POPSICLES

❀ Makes 4 • Prep 5' • Overnight freezing • Easy ❀

280ml Elbling or other
  white wine
60ml Cassero or
  blackcurrant liqueur
2 tsp icing sugar

In a jug, mix the white wine, blackcurrant liqueur and icing sugar.

Pour into 4 popsicle moulds, stick popsicle sticks into each and freeze overnight.

When ready to serve, remove the popsicle moulds from the freezer. Pop out the popsicles and serve immediately.

I often order a *Kir Royal* as an *aperitif*: sparkling wine sweetened with blackcurrant liqueur. This is my Luxembourg take on this classic tipple: a *Kir Royal* with *Quetschen*! I'm making an alcohol syrup with *Quetschegebeess*, damson jam, to pimp my Crémant. It's really easy to make and totally tastes of Luxembourg.

QUETSCHEN KIPPCHEN

❤ Serves 6 • Prep 15' • Cooling 30' • Easy ❤

8 tbsp damson jam
120ml vodka
2 damsons, to serve
1 bottle Crémant or
    sparkling wine

Put the damson jam into a saucepan with 2 tablespoons of the vodka. Put over a medium heat and stir until the jam is quite runny.

Strain through a sieve, discarding any solid bits. Mix the liquid with the remaining vodka and set aside to cool for 30 minutes.

Cut the damsons into quarters and remove the stone. Make a slit into each damson quarter and set aside.

Pour 2 tablespoons of damson vodka into each champagne glass and carefully top with Crémant or sparkling wine.

Decorate each glass with a damson quarter and serve.

TIP

Don't throw away the strained damson pieces – you can use them as a topping on a *Schmier* (slice of bread). Beware they're spiked with vodka, so you better not have this for breakfast!

In the UK, my neighbour Tom used to make sloe gin for Christmas. He would pick sloe berries in autumn, stuff them into a bottle of gin and let them infuse for a while, resulting in a flavoured gin like no other. I thought it would be fun to make a boozy infusion with a local ingredient from Luxembourg, too. Rhubarb immediately sprang to mind, as I'm obsessed with rhubarb!
No need to splash out on expensive vodka for this recipe, a cheap bottle will do the job.
The rhubarb vodka works well as an aperitif mixed with Crémant, or you can fill it into little bottles to give away as presents.

RHUBARB VODKA

❧ Makes 1 bottle • Prep 15' • Infusing 3 weeks • Easy ❧

800g rhubarb
225g sugar
750ml vodka

Trim the rhubarb, wash, pat dry and cut into cubes.

Put the rhubarb cubes into a large jar, add the sugar and the vodka.
Seal and shake.

Store the jar in a cool, dark place for 3 weeks and shake every few days.

After 3 weeks, strain the vodka into a bottle, discard the rhubarb pieces.
Store in the fridge as it tastes best ice cold.

Drink straight or use it as a basis for a spritzy rhubarb Kir Royal.

TIP

You can experiment with other vodka flavours. For example, you can add scraped out vanilla pods to the vodka, or whole cinnamon sticks for a festively spiced version.

One of my stand-by desserts consists of fruit compote, whipped cream and meringue brittle. All you need to do is arrange the various elements in layers in a pretty serving bowl, and that's your perfect dessert sorted. So simple yet so good!

RHUBARB MESS

❀ Makes 4 • Prep 30' • Cooling 1h • Easy ❀

For the rhubarb compote:
400g rhubarb
40g sugar
juice of ½ lemon
1 tbsp water
½ cinnamon stick

150ml cream
30g sugar
1 sachet vanilla sugar
150g yoghurt
4 meringues

Trim the rhubarb and cut into 1 cm cubes. Put into a saucepan together with the sugar, lemon juice, water and cinnamon stick. Cover with a lid and cook for about 8 minutes, stirring from time to time, until the rhubarb is soft.

After 8 minutes, uncover the rhubarb and cook for another 10 minutes, stirring from time to time, until you have a soft compote. Take off the heat and set aside. Remove the cinnamon stick, pour the compote into a bowl and leave to cool for 1 hour.

Meanwhile, whip the cream with the sugar and vanilla sugar until stiff. Fold in the yoghurt and refrigerate until needed.

Once the rhubarb is cool, put a spoonful of rhubarb compote at the bottom of 4 serving glasses.

Crush the meringues and put half the meringue brittle on top of the rhubarb compote. Top the meringue with half the cream, then add another layer of rhubarb followed by a layer of cream and finish with the remaining meringue brittle.

Serve immediately.

TIP

• You can prepare the compote up to 3 days ahead.
• This also tastes great with other fruit compotes like apple, apricot or damson.

This orange cream (without the cinnamon) was a well-kept family secret for a long time. My grandma would regularly make it as dessert for her Sunday lunch, and my mum has served it at many a dinner party. When I asked her for the recipe, she said she'd only give it to me if I promised not to share it on my blog or in any of my books. Now, I'm not one for breaking promises, but after years of me begging to publish it, my mum and grandma finally caved and allowed me to use it here. Needless to say I am really grateful for this and I have learnt one invaluable lesson: persistence pays off, yay!

SPICED ORANGE CREAM

❧ Serves 4 • Prep 30' • Cooling 2h • Easy ❧

2 eggs
120g sugar
1 tsp vanilla sugar
a pinch of cinnamon
3 oranges
½ lemon
160ml cream
2 tsp cornstarch

Crack the eggs into a saucepan and mix with the sugar, vanilla sugar and cinnamon.

Squeeze the juice from the oranges and lemon and pass through a sieve to remove any pulp.

Add the orange and lemon juice to the saucepan with the eggs and mix.

Mix 2 tbsp of cream with the cornstarch and add to the egg mix, whisking until the cornstarch has dissolved.

Place the saucepan over a medium heat, keep whisking and warm the liquid until it thickens.

Once the liquid has thickened and covers the back of a spoon, pour into a serving bowl and leave to cool.

Once it is completely cool, beat 150ml cream in a separate bowl until stiff. Fold the whipped cream into the cooled egg mix until you get a smooth mousse.

Distribute between four serving bowls, dust each portion with some cinnamon and serve with butter cookies.

TIPS

• This cream can be made with all kinds of fruit juices. Why not try it with regional apple or cherry juice next time?
• The cooked part can be prepared in advance, even the day before; simply add the whipped cream up to 2 hours before serving.

I absolutely adore tiramisu and I think it's fair to say that most Luxembourgers have a soft spot for this Italian dessert. This is my go-to recipe for tiramisu! I have replaced the Amaretto almond liqueur with Luxembourg walnut liqueur, making it a tad less sweet. And I top the whole thing with walnut brittle, which adds a crunchy finish.

NUTTY TIRAMISU

Serves 6 • Prep 30' • Cooling 4h • Easy

150ml coffee,
  sweetened with
  1 tbsp sugar
2 eggs
1 tbsp vanilla sugar
70g sugar
250g mascarpone
200ml cream
80ml walnut liqueur
175g sponge finger
  biscuits
cocoa powder,
  for dusting

For the walnut brittle:
60g sugar
60g walnuts

Start by making the coffee, add 1 tablespoon of sugar and leave to cool.

Separate the eggs. Beat the egg whites until stiff. In a large mixing bowl, beat the egg yolks with the vanilla sugar and sugar. Add the mascarpone and beat again.

Add the stiff egg whites to the mascarpone cream, but don't mix yet.

Pour the cream into the bowl used for the egg whites, whisk until stiff. Fold the whipped cream and the stiff egg whites into the mascarpone cream until smooth.

Mix the coffee with the walnut liqueur and pour into a deep plate.

Dip half of the biscuits in the coffee so that they soak up the liquid. Arrange them side-by-side at the base of a large dessert bowl. Spread half the mascarpone cream over the biscuits, then top with another layer of coffee-soaked biscuits and finish with a final layer of mascarpone cream.

Cover the dessert bowl with cling film and refrigerate for at least 4 hours, so the flavours can infuse.

Meanwhile, make the walnut brittle. Heat the sugar in a frying pan and melt. Leave the sugar bubbling until the caramel starts to turn light golden. Add the walnuts and stir so all the walnuts are covered in caramel. Pour the brittle onto a sheet of baking paper and leave to cool.

Once cool, fold the baking paper containing the walnuts into a little parcel and bash them to smaller pieces using a pestle, rolling pin or heavy object. Set aside.

Before serving, dust the tiramisu with cocoa powder and sprinkle with the walnut brittle.

Serve with a small glass of walnut liqueur.

Ask anyone who knows me and they'll tell you that I go crazy for meringues, and especially so for meringue and ice cream, which is my favourite combination in the world. So I obviously love a good vacherin for dessert! You're bound to impress your guests when you serve this patriotic vacherin for Luxembourg national day on the 23rd June!

PATRIOTIC VACHERIN

❋ 23 cm springform • Serves 8 • Prep 1h • Oven 1h 45' • Freezing 8h • Worth the effort ❋

For the meringue:
2 egg whites
a pinch of salt
100g sugar
blue food colouring

For the vanilla ice cream layer:
2 eggs
a pinch of salt
1 vanilla pod
100g sugar
250ml cream

For the strawberry ice cream layer:
250g strawberries
125g icing sugar
250ml cream
2 tsp lemon juice

For the decoration:
100ml cream
1 tbsp icing sugar
250g strawberries

For the meringue:
Preheat the oven to 120°C fan.

Put the egg whites into a bowl with a pinch of salt and beat with an electric whisk until they form soft peaks. Keep whisking and gradually add the sugar, 2 spoonfuls at a time, whisking for 20 to 30 seconds between each addition. Keep whisking until the sugar has dissolved and the meringue is stiff and shiny.

Dye the meringue with blue food colouring until it has the desired shade (you will need quite a lot!), whisking to evenly distribute the dye.

Place a 23cm springform onto a sheet of baking paper. Draw a circle around the inside of the springform with a pencil. Place the sheet of baking paper onto a baking tray and evenly distribute the meringue mix all over the circle drawn on the baking paper.

Bake the meringue for 1h 45 mins, then leave to cool on a wire rack. Once cool, put onto a piece of baking paper. Press the springform ring (without the bottom) onto the meringue, so the meringue becomes the bottom. Store any meringue brittle that may have fallen off the sides in a bowl and keep as decoration for later. Set aside.

For the vanilla ice cream layer:
Separate the eggs into two bowls. Add a pinch of salt to the egg whites and beat with an electric whisk until they form stiff peaks.

Slice the vanilla pod lengthwise and scrape out the seeds; add to the egg yolks with the sugar and whisk until pale.

Add the beaten egg whites to the egg yolks, but don't mix yet.

Pour the cream into the bowl used for the egg whites and beat until stiff.

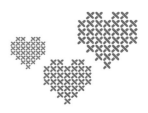

Add the whipped cream to the eggs and fold in gently until no big lumps are left. Don't overmix, as you want it to stay light and fluffy.

Spread the vanilla ice cream evenly over the meringue, cover the surface with cling film and freeze for at least 4 hours.

For the strawberry ice cream layer:
Once the vanilla ice cream layer has set, make the strawberry ice cream layer.

Wash and trim the strawberries and put into a blender with the icing sugar, cream and lemon juice. Blend into a purée.

Put the purée into an ice cream maker and churn until it has thickened.

Remove the cling film from the vanilla ice cream layer and spread the strawberry ice cream evenly over the vanilla ice cream. Cover the surface with cling film and freeze again for at least 4 hours.

When ready to serve, wash the strawberries, trim and cut into halves.

Whip the cream with the icing sugar until stiff. Put into a piping bag fitted with a star-shaped nozzle.

Take the spring form out of the freezer and leave at room temperature for 10 minutes until the ring comes off easily (you can cut around the edges if it sticks).

Put the vacherin onto a cake plate and decorate with the strawberry halves, a circle of whipped cream and blue meringue brittle. Serve immediately.

TIPS
- You can bake the meringue the day before making the ice cream.
- This vacherin keeps in the freezer for 1 month without the strawberries and whipped cream topping – add these just before serving.
- With the leftover egg yolk, you could make *pastéis de nata* (page 254).

My parents have a little pear tree in their garden and a few years ago it yielded a huge crop. We were running out of ideas of what to do with the pears: from pear cakes to pear compote, pear sorbet and pear clafoutis, we had worked our way through every recipe we could think of. I can tell that we'll have just as many pears again this year, so as a preventative measure, I have created this new recipe: my take on the lovely *Poire Belle Hélène*. Is there anything tastier than the combination of pears and dark chocolate? It turns out there is: pears, dark chocolate, ginger and lime zest! Trust me, you'll never go back to traditional *Poire Belle Hélène* again!

POIRE BELLE HÉLÈNE MY WAY

❀ Serves 4 • Prep 45' • Easy ❀

800ml water
220g sugar
1 vanilla pod
4 Conference pears

For the chocolate sauce:
40g crystalized ginger
110g dark chocolate
100ml cream
zest of 1 lime, grated

vanilla ice cream,
to serve

Start by making a sugar syrup: put the water and sugar into a saucepan large enough to fit the pears snuggled side by side. Slice open the vanilla pod lengthwise and add to the saucepan. Put over a medium heat until the sugar has dissolved, stirring from time to time.

Meanwhile, remove a little of the core from the base of each pear by cutting into the stem at the base with a small, pointy knife. Peel the pears using a vegetable peeler, leaving the stem intact. Cut off the bottom, so the pears can stand upright when you serve them.

Place the pears into the sugar syrup so it's a snuggly fit. Cover with a lid and cook for approximately 20 minutes, turning the pears regularly to make them soak up the sugar syrup on all sides. The pears are done when they can be pierced easily with a knife – the cooking time depends on the ripeness of the pears.

When the pears are done, take off the heat and leave them in the sugar syrup while preparing the chocolate sauce.

Cut the crystalized ginger into small dice. Break the chocolate into chunks and put into a saucepan with the cream. Melt into a smooth sauce while stirring and add the crystalized ginger cubes shortly before serving.

Distribute the pears between 4 plates, pour over some of the chocolate sauce and sprinkle with grated lime zest. Serve with vanilla ice cream.

TIP

You can make *gingembrettes* with the leftover crystalized ginger. Simply cut the ginger into slices and dip into melted dark chocolate. Leave to cool on a piece of baking paper and enjoy alongside a cup of coffee.

I think most people who grew up in Luxembourg have fond memories of their grandmothers making *Gebaken Äppel* in autumn. Apples are cored and stuffed with raisins, sugar, cinnamon and butter and baked until they're really soft. This recipe is a hybrid between a traditional *Gebakenen Apel* and an apple pie. The apples are filled with an apple pie stuffing and then topped with a pretty pastry lid. They're fun to make and really quite cute.

BAKED APPLES

❀ Makes 8 • Prep 1h • Fridge 1h • Oven 25' • A little effort ❀

For the dough:
100g cold butter
150g flour
30g icing sugar
a pinch of salt
1 egg
1 tbsp cold water

For the apples:
40g raisins
1 tbsp rum
8 apples (Jonagold)
40g almond flakes
100g brown sugar
cinnamon
20g butter

Start by making the dough. Cut the butter into small cubes and put into a large bowl together with the flour, icing sugar and a pinch of salt. Rub between your fingers until it resembles breadcrumbs.

Separate the egg and add the egg yolk to the dough. Keep the egg white for brushing the pastry before it goes into the oven.

Add 1 tablespoon of cold water to the bowl and knead into a dough. Shape the dough into a disc and wrap in cling film. Refrigerate for 1 hour.

While the dough is in the fridge, put the raisins into a small bowl and soak in the rum.

Once the dough is chilled, preheat the oven to 180°C fan.

Cut a 1 cm 'lid' off the top of each apple. Peel the lids and cut the flesh into small cubes. Put the apple cubes into a bowl. Add the almond flakes, sugar, soaked raisins and a bit of cinnamon to taste. Mix and set the filling aside.

Using a teaspoon, scrape out the inside of the apples, leaving a border of approximately 1 cm and stopping halfway down. Stuff the apples with the filling, sticking a small piece of butter into the centre. Place the stuffed apples into the holes of a muffin tin.

Cut the chilled dough into 8 equal pieces. Roll out one piece on a floured surface until really thin. Cut into a square shape, then cut the square into 6 strips.

To make a lattice, lay out 3 strips vertically in front of you, spacing them a little apart. Fold the 2 outer strips back on themselves. Place a new strip horizontally to the vertical strips over the middle strip. Unfold the folded vertical strips over the new horizontal strip. Now fold the middle strip running underneath the horizontal strip back over the horizontal strip. Place another horizontal strip over the vertical strips and unfold the middle strip. Repeat this weaving process one last time so you end up with a lattice square.

Place the pastry lattice on top of an apple like a lid. Repeat with the remaining dough.

Once all the apples have a pastry lid, brush each lattice with the egg white. Put the muffin tin into the preheated oven and bake for 25 minutes. Serve the apples warm.

Damson season is quite a big deal in Luxembourg. There are *Quetschefester* (damson fêtes) taking place throughout the country where you can sometimes see how they cook *Quetschekraut* (damson 'kraut', a jam of sorts) the old-fashioned way in huge copper caldrons. I always make sure I eat lots of *Quetschentaart* (damson tart) while the fruit is in season – a simple yeast dough topped with damson quarters and dusted with icing sugar just before serving. Both my previous books feature recipes for damson tart, so I thought it was time to shake things up a bit. Here's a recipe that shows off the versatility of the humble damson. It's perfect for surprising your guests with something unusual and unexpected. Plus, it can be whipped up in only an hour.

RED WINE DAMSONS WITH FINANCIERS

For the financiers: Makes 12 financiers • Prep 25' • Oven 18' • Easy
For the red wine damsons: Serves 4 • Prep 30' • Easy

For the financiers:
65g butter + extra for greasing
6 firm damsons
50g ground almonds
150g sugar
50g flour
4 egg whites
a pinch of salt

For the red wine damsons:
500g damsons
150ml red wine
75g sugar
1 star anise
a shot of damson schnapps (optional)

vanilla ice cream, to serve

For the financiers:
Preheat the oven to 180°C fan.

Grease 12 holes of a muffin tin.

Wash the damsons and pat dry. Cut into quarters, removing the stone, and set aside.

Put the ground almonds, sugar, flour and egg whites into a bowl with a pinch of salt. Whisk until you get an even batter.

Melt the butter in a small saucepan and cook for approximately 5 minutes until it starts to brown and has a nutty smell. Take off the hob and pour the hot butter into the batter while whisking, leaving any brown bits at the bottom of the saucepan.

Distribute the batter between the 12 muffin holes, filling them halfway, and stick 2 damson quarters into each muffin hole.

Bake in the preheated oven for 18 minutes. Put the tin on a wire rack, leave to cool for 5 minutes before carefully unmolding the financiers. These are best eaten on the day they are baked.

For the red wine damsons:
Wash the damsons, cut into quarters and remove the stone. Put into a saucepan.

Add the red wine, sugar and star anise, cover and put over a medium heat. Cook for 12 minutes, stirring regularly, until the fruit is soft. Set aside to cool for 10 minutes and add a shot of damson schnapps before serving.

These stewed damsons can be eaten warm or cold with vanilla ice cream on the side.

This dessert is very quick and easy to make, yet it looks extremely pretty and impressive.
The perfect showstopper for a summer dinner party!

RASPBERRY & BLUEBERRY 'MILLE-FEUILLE'

❤ Serves 4 • Prep 20' • Quick & Easy ❤

½ vanilla pod
100ml cream
1 tbsp icing sugar
125g raspberries
125g blueberries
8 thin butter wafers

Slice the vanilla pod lengthwise and scrape out the seeds.

Whip the cream with the icing sugar and the vanilla seeds until stiff.
Put into a piping bag fitted with a round nozzle.

Wash the raspberries and blueberries and pat dry.

Distribute 4 wafers between 4 plates. Place a raspberry onto a wafer then pipe
a dollop of whipped cream next to it, followed by a blueberry.

Keep alternating between whipped cream and fruit until the entire wafer is
covered.

Top with a second wafer and repeat the process.

Serve immediately.

TIPS

• You can make this recipe with strawberries or with blackberries, too.
• If you want to make the butter wafers yourself, use my recipe from page 245.

These truffles were inspired by a trip to Warsaw. At the airport, on my way home, I bought a little bag of white chocolate covered almonds, which were dusted with cinnamon. I was in heaven! So, as I sat on the plane popping almond after almond into my mouth, I started thinking of a recipe that would play with these heavenly flavours. That's how, pretty quickly, these boozy truffles were born. They combine white chocolate, cinnamon and honey schnapps and are covered in crunchy roast almond brittle. Be warned, they do have a kick to them and I suggest you keep them out of reach of children, who would no doubt find them just as addictive as any adult with a sweet tooth.

HONEY SCHNAPPS TRUFFLES

Makes 25 • Prep 30' • Cooling 3h • Easy

200g white chocolate
20g butter
40ml honey schnapps
½ tsp cinnamon

For the almond brittle:
40g sugar
40g flaked almonds

Break the chocolate into chunks. Melt the butter in a saucepan placed over a water bath and add the chocolate, stirring constantly so that it melts completely.

Add the honey schnapps and the cinnamon and melt into a smooth ganache. The mix may split at first, so that it looks like the butter doesn't mix with the rest – this will change once it is heated through. Do not cook the ganache for too long though, or the alcohol will evaporate.

Pour the ganache into a bowl and leave to cool for 15 minutes. Cover with cling film and refrigerate for 2 hours.

Meanwhile, make the almond brittle: heat the sugar in a frying pan until the sugar melts. Leave the sugar bubbling until the caramel starts to turn light golden. Add the almonds and stir until all the almonds are covered in caramel. Pour the almond brittle onto a sheet of baking paper and leave to cool.

Once cool, fold the baking paper containing the almonds into a little parcel and bash the almonds into smaller pieces using a pestle, rolling pin or other heavy object until you get a fine brittle. Put the brittle on a plate and set aside.

Once the ganache has set, take a teaspoon of ganache (it will have the texture of marzipan), shape it into a little hazelnut-sized ball between your hands and roll it in the almond brittle. Repeat until the ganache is used up.

Put all the truffles on a plate and cover with cling film. Refrigerate briefly so they can firm up.

These truffles can be stored in the fridge for 2 weeks.

 TIP If you have got some almond brittle left, don't throw it away: you can use it as a delicious ice-cream topping!

I know lots of people in Luxembourg who have redcurrant bushes in their gardens. The easiest way to use up large amounts of redcurrants is to make jelly with them! I decided to make mine with a hint of rosemary – it's great on a slice of buttered bread or on some cottage cheese. The depth of flavor of the rosemary makes this jelly quite versatile as you can serve a dollop as a side with game or even add a spoonful to a meaty red wine sauce for a good balance of flavours. Redcurrants are naturally high in pectin, the fruit sugar that makes jelly or jam set. So you won't need to buy special jam sugar with added pectin to make this redcurrant jelly.

REDCURRANT JELLY

❀ Makes 4 jam jars • Prep 1h • Easy ❀

1.4kg redcurrants
2 rosemary sprigs
1.4kg sugar
a shot of Kirsch
(optional)

Start by sterilizing 4 jam jars. Preheat the oven to 180°C fan.

Wash the jam jars and lids and put them onto a clean tea towel, facing upwards. Once the oven is hot, put the jars onto a baking tray and put into the oven for 10 minutes. Then turn off the oven and leave the glasses inside until ready to fill. Meanwhile, bring a saucepan with water to the boil and boil the metal lids for 10 minutes, putting them on the clean tea towel to dry. Don't be tempted to dry the lids with the tea towel, they should dry in the air.

For the jelly :
Wash the redcurrants and put them into a large, heavy-bottomed saucepan, stalks on. Add the rosemary sprigs and a bit of water so the bottom of the saucepan is covered.

Put on a high heat and cook the redcurrants for 10 minutes, stirring regularly and pressing the berries from time to time so that they release their juices.

After 10 minutes, add the sugar, stir until dissolved and bring to the boil. Cook the fruit for 7 minutes.

Put a fine mesh sieve over a bowl.

After 7 minutes, take the fruit off the hob and (if using) add a shot of Kirsch and stir.

Pour a few ladles of the redcurrants into the sieve, pressing down with the ladle to release as much as juice as possible. Discard the pulp and stalks and repeat until all the redcurrants have been pressed.

Fill the hot jelly into the jam jars, close the lids tightly and put upside down onto a wire rack. Leave to cool completely before turning the jam jars over. To test if a vacuum seal has formed in the jars, you can press down the middle of the lid – if the lid springs back when you release the pressure, it's not fully sealed and will only keep for a few weeks in the fridge. If the seal is tight, the jelly will keep in a dark, cool place for a at least 1 year.

You can't imagine my excitement when I was given a 3D-printed cookie cutter in the shape of Luxembourg! What a brilliant gimmick, and perfect for this book! You can of course make these cookies with any kind of cookie cutter, patriotic or not, they will always taste of home due to their honey schnapps-spiked icing. The cookie dough is also an excellent base for any flavoured sugar cookie: around Christmas time you can add cinnamon to the dough, or a sprinkle of grated lime zest to the icing.

LUXEMBOURG COOKIES

Makes 85 cookies • Prep 1h15' • Cooling 30' • Oven 10' per batch • A little effort

250g butter,
  room temperature
140g icing sugar
1 sachet vanilla sugar
1 vanilla pod
1 egg
375g flour
a pinch of salt

For the icing:
120g icing sugar
4 ½ tsp honey schnapps
red + blue food colouring

Cut the butter into cubes and put in a mixing bowl together with the icing sugar and vanilla sugar and mix.

Slice the vanilla pod lengthwise, scrape out the seeds, add them to the bowl and mix.

Add the egg and mix again, then add the flour and salt and beat into a smooth dough.

Flatten the dough into two discs, wrap in cling film and refrigerate for 30 minutes.

After 30 minutes, preheat the oven to 170°C fan.

Roll out the chilled dough on a surface dusted with flour. Cut out cookies with a 7cm cookie cutter and place on a baking tray lined with baking paper.

Bake in the preheated oven for 10 minutes or until browned at the edges. Put onto a wire rack and leave to cool completely.

Once the cookies are cool, prepare the icing. Put 40g of icing sugar into a small bowl, add 1 ½ tablespoons of honey schnapps and a few drops of red food colouring and mix into a smooth icing. Decorate ⅓ of the cookies with the red icing.

Repeat the same process with the blue food colouring, then mix the remaining icing sugar with the remaining honey schnapps to create the white icing.

Leave the iced cookies to set for at least 1 hour.

The cookies will keep in a tin for at least 1 week.

TIP

You can replace the honey schnapps with lemon juice or milk for an alcohol-free treat.

I think many Luxembourgers have fond memories of making *Wäffelcher* at their grandparents'. These thin, buttery wafers are baked individually in a round waffle maker, then wrapped around the handle of a wooden spoon while still hot, so that they get a cone shape. While I was rolling *Wäffelcher* for this book, I suddenly thought it would be really fun to fold them into fortune cookies instead and hide messages inside! I also jazzed up the traditional recipe by adding black sesame seeds to the batter – the inspiration for this comes from a trip to Thailand, where I once ate thin coconut-flavoured wafers specked with black sesame seeds and rolled up just like in Luxembourg. My favourite treat from Luxembourg with an Asian twist!

FORTUNE COOKIE WÄFFELCHER

❧ Makes 25 • Prep 45' • Resting 30' • A little effort ❧

2 eggs
85g sugar
1 tsp vanilla sugar
85g butter, melted +
 extra for greasing
85g flour
a pinch of salt
½ tsp black sesame
 seeds (optional)
25 paper messages, to
 stick into the cookies

Put the eggs into a bowl and whisk together with the sugar and vanilla sugar. Add the melted butter, whisk again, then add the flour, salt and sesame seeds and beat to a smooth batter. Set aside to rest at room temperature for 30 minutes. This will make the batter less runny.

After 30 minutes, switch on a round waffle iron. Butter the iron, then pour a heaped teaspoon of batter into the centre. Close and bake the wafer until golden (every waffle maker is different, it can take between 30 seconds and 2 minutes, just open it from time to time to peek inside).

Now you need to work quickly: remove the wafer with a spatula, and put onto a wire rack. Place a fortune in the centre of the wafer. Quickly fold the wafer in half, then fold the two edges towards each other so that you get a crescent shape. This needs to be done really fast because the wafer will harden and become brittle within seconds.

Place the folded fortune cookie into a muffin tin so it hold its shape as it cools. Leave to cool completely, then store in a tin for up to a week.

TIPS

• The diameter of a traditional *Wäffelchen* is about 15cm. As these are fortune cookie wafers, you'll want the wafer to be on the small side. The diameter I aim for is about 12cm, as the wafers are easier to fold when they're small.

• It's very likely that you'll burn your fingers while shaping the fortune cookies... My solution is to wrap both my thumbs and index fingers in foil so I can't feel the heat. It may look very odd, but it is a very handy trick indeed!

• You can find plenty of printable fortune cookie messages online.

• Black sesame seeds are available in Asian supermarkets. They are a bit crunchier than white sesame seeds, but their taste is very similar. You can of course use white sesame seeds in this recipe.

Schuedi is a humble Luxembourgish yeast cake, which is specked with buttery, sugar-filled holes. 'Schued' means 'a shame' or 'a pity' in Luxembourgish, so *Schuedi* could be translated as 'a pity of a cake', which is completely misleading as it's a cake that you really don't need to be ashamed of. The reason why this cake is called *Schuedi* is a different one: People used to make it with leftover yeast dough after making bread, as it would have been a pity, or 'schued', to throw the excess dough away. My *Schuedi* comes with a combination of butter and jam holes, making it the perfect breakfast cake.

BUTTERY JAM SCHUEDI

❁ For a 23 cm tart tin • Prep 30' • Resting 1h30' • Oven 25' • Easy ❁

260g flour
21g fresh yeast
125ml lukewarm milk
90g sugar
100g butter
1 sachet vanilla sugar
1 egg
a pinch of salt
a few tablespoons
   of jam

For the 'starter', put the flour into a large mixing bowl and make a well in the centre. Crumble the yeast into a jar and mix with the lukewarm milk and 1 teaspoon of sugar until diluted. Pour the yeasty milk into the well, making sure that the liquid doesn't spill too far out of the well.

Stir the milk mix inside the well with a bit of flour from the sides so that you get a loose dough. Sprinkle with a bit of flour from the sides of the well. Cover the bowl with a damp tea towel and leave to rise at room temperature for 15 minutes.

After the 15 minutes, cut 40g of butter into cubes. Add 40g of sugar, half the vanilla sugar, the cubed butter, the egg and salt to the 'starter' and mix with the kneading attachment of an electric hand or stand mixer. Work into a smooth dough, using your hands if necessary. Cover the bowl with the tea towel and leave to rise at room temperature for 45 minutes so the dough doubles in size.

Grease a 23 cm tart tin and dust with flour.

After 45 minutes, take the dough out of the bowl and put onto a floured surface. Knock the dough back by briefly kneading it, then roll into a disc the size of the tart tin. Lift into the tin, cover with the tea towel and leave to rest for another 30 minutes.

Shortly before the 30 minutes are over, preheat the oven to 160°C fan.

Cut 40g of butter into 1cm cubes. Mix the remaining 50g sugar with the remaining vanilla sugar.

Uncover the dough and, using your thumb, poke holes all over the cake surface. Stuff half of the cake holes with ¼ tsp of sugar and 1 butter cube each. Fill the remaining holes with jam.

Melt the remaining 20g of butter and use it to brush the entire cake surface. Sprinkle the cake with the remaining sugar and bake in the preheated oven for 25 minutes.

Turn onto a wire rack and leave to cool – you can already eat it when it's still a bit warm but it's just as delicious once cooled.

Marmorkuch is one of those cakes that every Luxembourger must have grown up with! I vividly remember eating it during my childhood at most play-dates with my friends. We would come back home from building huts, riding our rollerblades or causing general mischief and find a *Marmorkuch* waiting for us in the kitchen (be it at mine or theirs – everyone used to make marble cake back in the day). This specific *Marmorkuch* is not as dry as the classic version. I made it with chocolate-hazelnut-spread and I've given it a two-tone icing to mirror the colours at play inside this delicious cake.

MY MARBLE CAKE

❀ 20x10cm loaf tin • Makes 1 loaf • Prep 45' • Oven 1h • Easy ❀

For the cake:
250g butter, room
   temperature
180g sugar
1 vanilla pod
3 eggs
250g flour
3 tsp baking powder
a pinch of salt
80g chocolate-
   hazelnut-spread
4 tsp cocoa powder

For the white icing:
30g butter, room
   temperature
60g cream cheese
120g icing sugar

For the brown icing:
50g butter, room
   temperature
50g chocolate-
   hazelnut-spread
40g icing sugar
1 tsp cocoa powder

Preheat the oven to 170°C fan.

Butter a rectangular cake tin (20x10cm) and set aside.

Cut the butter into small cubes, put into a bowl with the sugar and beat until fluffy.

Slice open the vanilla pod, scrape out the seeds and add them to the bowl.

Add the eggs to the bowl and beat again.

In a separate bowl, mix the flour, baking powder and a pinch of salt and gradually add into the butter mix until well incorporated.

Cover the bottom of the cake tin with 400g of the batter.

Add the chocolate-hazelnut-spread and cocoa powder to the remaining batter and mix until well incorporated.

Cover the white batter in the cake tin with the chocolate batter. Using a fork, cut into the batter while making a spiral movement from one side to the other - this will create the marble pattern. Repeat the movement all along the entire length of the cake to get a pattern throughout.

Bake the cake in the preheated oven for 1 hour. Take out of the tin and leave to cool on a wire rack.

Once the cake is cool, prepare the 2 icings. Mix all the ingredients for the white icing in one bowl and the ingredients for the brown icing in another bowl. Put both icings into separate piping bags. Fit a third large piping bag with a star-shaped nozzle and place the 2 filled piping bags into the large piping bag, so that the open tips both fit inside the star nozzle. Test your icing by piping a dollop onto a plate. Both colours should be visible; if they aren not, rearrange the 2 piping bags inside the and try again.

Pipe little dollops of icing onto the cake until the top of the cake is completely covered. Serve the cake immediately or keep the iced cake in the fridge until needed.

I can't think of anything more exciting than rhubarb. Yes, apples make me happy, raspberries are a sheer delight and pineapple is just gorgeous, but nothing is more thrilling than rhubarb. Maybe it's because its season is so short and its arrival means it's springtime. Or maybe it's because I am absolutely crazy about rhubarb tarts! Though they often have one major flaw: a soggy bottom! Indeed, the rhubarb's juices have a tendency to spoil the crispy tart case and make it go all sludgy. Not mine! The trick is to drain the liquid from the rhubarb before baking the tarts. That means you have to start a day in advance, but the crispy base is well worth it!

RHUBARB TARTELETTES

Makes 10 tartelettes of 10 cm • Prep 1h 30' • Marinating overnight • Oven 40' • A little effort

1kg rhubarb
80g sugar
1 tsp cinnamon

For the pastry:
125g butter, cold
60g icing sugar
250g flour
1 egg
3 tbsp cold water
a pinch of salt

For the custard:
150ml cream
110g sugar
1 sachet vanilla sugar
3 eggs

The day before baking the tartelettes, wash, trim and peel the rhubarb so you're left with about 800g. Cut into small cubes and put into a bowl. Mix the sugar with the cinnamon and sprinkle over the rhubarb. Mix so the rhubarb is evenly coated. Put into a colander and place over a bowl, to catch the rhubarb juices. Refrigerate overnight.

The next day, prepare the pastry. Cut the butter into cubes and put into a bowl with the icing sugar. Mix with an electric mixer fitted with a kneading attachment. Add the flour, egg, water and a pinch of salt and mix until the dough comes together. Shape into a disc, cover in cling film and refrigerate for 30 minutes.

Meanwhile, make the custard. In a jug, mix the cream, sugar, vanilla sugar and eggs. Refrigerate until later.

Grease the tart tins.

Preheat the oven to 170°C fan.

Take the rhubarb out of the fridge and discard the juices.

Take the dough out of the fridge and roll out thinly on a floured surface. Cut out discs large enough to fill the tart tins and lift them into the tart tins. Press the dough firmly against the rims to make it stick.

Fill the pastry cases with rhubarb so the bottom is evenly covered. Pour some custard over the rhubarb so it fills the entire pastry case.

Bake the tartelettes in the preheated oven for 40 minutes. Take out of the tins while still hot, put onto a wire rack and leave to cool completely before serving.

TIP

You can make these tarts with other fruit, too: mirabelles, blueberries, cherries, apples or damsons work equally well.

I could not write this book and not include at least one scrumptious, buttery autumnal cake. While I often make apple cakes once the leaves start to turn, I thought it would be nice to jazz it up and go for a pear topping instead. You can of course make this recipe with apples, or with a mix of apples and pears.

BUTTERY PEAR CAKE

❀ 23cm spring form • Prep 30' • Oven 50' • Easy ❀

For the pears:
3 pears
50g butter
2 tbsp sugar
1 vanilla pod

For the cake:
180g butter, soft
140g sugar
3 eggs
100g ground almonds
100g flour
1½ tsp baking powder
½ tsp cinnamon
a pinch of nutmeg
a pinch of salt
2 tbsp quince jelly

Preheat the oven to 170°C fan.

Wash the pears, quarter and core, then halve the quarters lengthwise.

Melt the butter in a frying pan. Add the sugar and cook for a few minutes until the sugar starts to dissolve.

Slice the vanilla pod lengthwise and scrape out the seeds. Add the seeds and the vanilla pod to the butter, give it a swirl, then add the pear slices.

Cook the pears for 3 minutes, turning them halfway through. After 3 minutes, put the pears onto a plate, discard the vanilla pod and set the pan with the remaining juices aside for later.

Grease a 23cm spring form tin and line the bottom with baking paper.

In a large bowl, whisk the butter and the sugar until pale. Add the eggs one at a time, and whisk again.

In a separate bowl, mix the ground almonds, flour, baking powder and cinnamon with a pinch of nutmeg and salt. Gradually whisk the dry ingredients into the egg mix.

Distribute the batter in the spring form, then arrange the pears on top in a fan pattern.

Bake the cake for 50 minutes.

Just before the cake is done, put the frying pan with the pear juices back on the hob, bring the juices to the boil and reduce until they are sticky like caramel sauce.

When the cake is done, put the tin onto a wire rack and pour the pear caramel over the top. Leave to cool completely.

Once the cake is completely cool, take it out of the tin. Melt the quince jelly and use it to brush the pear topping to give it a lovely shine.

There is a large and vibrant Portuguese community in Luxembourg, so it's no surprise to find *Pastéis de Nata* in local bakeries: flaky, buttery pastries that encase a lovely vanilla pudding. My version of these Portuguese treats comes with a fruity little twist: a dollop of apple compote nestled underneath the custard, at the bottom of the tart case.

APPLE PASTÉIS DE NATA

❀ Makes 10 • Prep 50' • Cooling 1h • Easy ❀

2 egg yolks
35g sugar
1 tsp vanilla sugar
1 tbsp cornstarch
1 vanilla pod
100ml milk
100ml cream

butter, for greasing
230g all butter puff
  pastry
2 tbsp icing sugar
a small jar of apple
  compote
cinnamon, to dust

Start by making the custard. Combine the egg yolks, sugar, vanilla sugar and cornstarch in a bowl and mix.

Slice open the vanilla pod, scrape out the seeds and put both into a saucepan with the milk and the cream. Gently heat the liquid until nearly boiling. Remove the vanilla pod.

Slowly pour the hot liquid into the egg mixture, whisking vigorously in order not to curdle the eggs. Pour back into the saucepan and put over a medium heat, stirring constantly, until it starts to thicken and covers the back of a spoon.

Pour the custard into a bowl and leave to cool for 1 hour.

After 1 hour, preheat the oven to 200°C fan. Grease the holes of a muffin tin.

Unroll the puff pastry and dust with 2 tablespoons of icing sugar, distributing the sugar evenly over the puff pastry disc. Roll the puff pastry back onto itself and cut into 10 slices.

Place the pastry slices cut-side down onto a piece of baking paper, cover with another piece of baking paper and roll into discs big enough to line your muffin holes. Line the 10 muffin cases with the pastry, pricking the base with a fork.

Put 1 teaspoon of apple compote into each puff pastry case, then top with custard, leaving a 1cm margin below the top as the custard will rise significantly in the oven.

Bake the pastries in the preheated oven for 25 minutes. Take them out of the muffin tin and leave to cool on a wire rack. When cool, dust with cinnamon and serve at room temperature.

TIP   The tarts will keep in an airtight box for up to 2 days. If they soften, crisp them up in a medium oven for 5 minutes.

Bamkuch is reserved for life's major occasions, and it has a special place in every Luxembourger's heart. I had a big *Bamkuch* for my first Holy Communion and it is the country's most popular wedding cake. Its name translates as 'tree cake' because, when the classic log-shaped version is cut open, you see the baked rings like the rings of a tree trunk. Making *Bamkuch* the traditional way at home is virtually impossible, unless you happen to have a horizontal spit in your kitchen: the cake is made by drizzling batter onto the spinning spit, grilling layer after layer. There are two ways to make my *Bamkuch* in a normal oven: you can grill the cake layers under the oven grill, but I find it easier to control the baking process by baking the individual layers first before adding the characteristic grill marks with the help of a blow torch. I serve my *Bamkuch* in neat square-shaped bites, but if you want to do it the traditional way, cut the cake into very thin, delicate slices.

BAMKUCH

❀ For 1 rectangular cake tray measuring 25x20cm • Makes approx. 48 small squares ❀
❀ Prep 1h 15' • Worth the effort ❀

250g butter, soft +
   extra to grease
6 eggs
1 pinch salt
250g sugar
1 sachet vanilla sugar
5 tbsp rum
200g flour
50g cornstarch
2 tsp baking powder

For the layers:
1 ½ tbsp sugar
75ml water
1 ½ tbsp rum
3 tbsp apricot jam

For the icing:
180g icing sugar
2 tbsp rum
2 tbsp water

Preheat the oven to 180°C fan.

Grease a 25x20cm cake tin and line the base with baking paper.

Separate 4 eggs, putting the whites into a large bowl and the yolks into a small bowl.

Add a pinch of salt to the egg whites and beat until stiff.

In a large bowl, beat the butter, sugar and vanilla sugar. Add the 4 egg yolks and beat, then add the remaining two whole eggs and beat again. Add the rum and beat some more.

In a separate bowl, mix the flour, cornstarch and baking powder. Gradually add the flour mix to the butter mix, beating between additions.

Fold in the stiff egg whites with a spatula until you get an even, aerated batter.

Spread a thin, even layer of batter onto the base of the cake tin and bake the batter for 4 minutes until the it has set.

Meanwhile, put 1½ tbsp sugar, 75ml water and 1½ tbsp rum into a small saucepan and heat until all the sugar has dissolved.

Heat up the apricot jam in a separate saucepan so it becomes runny.

Take the cake tin out of the oven and char the surface with a blowtorch. Brush the surface with some apricot jam, then add another thin, even layer of batter. Bake for another 4 minutes until it has set.

Once the second layer is baked, char the surface again with the blowtorch, then drizzle some of the rum syrup over the cake with a small spoon – this needs to be done evenly, while making sure not to pour too much liquid over the cake.

Spread another layer of batter on top of the cake, pop into the oven for 4 minutes, char with the blowtorch and brush with apricot jam. Repeat this process until all the batter is used up – alternating between apricot jam and syrup layers.

Once you get to the last layer, bake this one for 10 minutes to make sure the cake is fully baked. Take out of the oven, char with the blowtorch but don't add any syrup or apricot jam this time.

Leave the cake to cool in its tin for 15 minutes. Turn out onto a wire rack and leave to cool completely.

Once the cake is cool, prepare the icing by mixing all the ingredients together in a small bowl. Spread over the top of the cake and leave to set.

Once the icing has set, cut the cake into squares and serve.

This cake keeps wrapped in foil for 4 days.

TIPS

• If you want to use the grill method instead of the blowtorch one, preheat your oven grill to high without turning on the actual oven. Grill each cake layer just below the grill for about 3 minutes until the top has browned. Alternate between apricot jam and rum syrup, just like in the recipe. At the end, heat the oven to 180°C fan and bake the cake for 10-15 minutes to ensure it is fully baked.

• Since it's quite labour-intensive to make this cake, it's worth baking 2 cakes at the same time. While one layer is baking in the oven, you prepare the next layer for the second cake, alternating between the 2 tins.

• You can freeze the uniced *Bamkuch* and ice it once it's completely defrosted.

I distinctly remember not liking *Fuesend* very much as a child. The obligation to dress up and dance with dodgy looking clowns at the local *Fuesbaal* was not my idea of fun. Still, I looked forward to *Fuesend* every year because this would be the time that my mum would make *Verwuerelter*. My sister and I always got very excited when Mum brought up the deep-fat fryer from the basement; that's when we knew we would be in for a treat. I'm really happy that my mum has agreed to share her recipe in this book. It really is the best one out there. Take my word for it!

VERWUERELTER

❧ Makes 45 • Prep 1h • Resting 2h • A little effort ❧

500g flour
42g fresh yeast
120g sugar
125ml milk, lukewarm
80g butter, room
   temperature
2 eggs
¼ tsp salt
40ml rum
2kg fat for deep-frying

To serve:
icing sugar
cinnamon
damson jam
   (Quetschekraut)

For the 'starter', put the flour into a large mixing bowl and make a well in the centre. Crumble the yeast into a jar and mix with the lukewarm milk and 1 tablespoon of sugar until diluted. Pour the yeasty milk into the well, making sure that the liquid doesn't spill too far out of the well.

Stir the milk mix inside the well with a bit of flour from the sides so that you get a loose dough. Sprinkle with a bit of flour from the sides of the well.

Cover the bowl with a damp tea towel and leave to rise at room temperature for 30 minutes.

After the 30 minutes, add the remaining sugar, butter, eggs and salt to the 'starter' and mix with the kneading attachment of an electric hand or stand mixer. Once the dough starts to come together, add the rum and work into a smooth dough, using your hands if needed.

Cover the bowl with the tea towel and leave to rise at room temperature for 1 hour.

After 1 hour, take the dough out of the bowl and put on a floured surface. Knock the dough back by briefly kneading it, then roll out to 1 cm thick.

Cut the dough into long strips of approximately 10 x 2 cm. Tie each strip into a loose knot and place onto a baking tray. Cover the knots with a dry tea towel and leave to rise at room temperature for 30 minutes.

While the knots are rising, heat the oil to 180°C in a deep-fat fryer (without the basket) or in a deep saucepan.

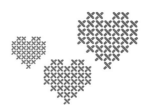

Fry the knots in batches so the fryer does not get overcrowded and there is enough room for all the knots to float on the surface. Fry for 1 ½ to 2 minutes on one side until well browned, then turn them over to brown the other side.

Remove the baked knots with a slotted spoon and put onto kitchen paper to drain some of the oil.

Just before serving, mix the icing sugar with some cinnamon and sprinkle over the Verwuerelter. Serve with damson jam on the side.

TIPS

• There are lots of different deep-frying oils and fats around and they will influence the taste of the final product. I find that Solo deep-frying fat tastes best.
• These *Verwuerelter* freeze incredibly well. Just freeze them on the day of making without the icing sugar and reheat them in the microwave for a few seconds.

You'd think that after a month of festive eating, people would feel like taking it easy in January. Nope. On the 6th January, Luxembourg celebrates *Dräikinneksdag* (Epiphany) by tucking into buttery *Galettes des Rois*. Each frangipane-stuffed puff pastry tart comes with a 'bean' hidden inside (usually a ceramic token). The person who gets the slice with the bean is crowned king or queen for a day. I have jazzed up the traditional *Galette des Rois* by making it miniature-sized and adding juicy cherries to the frangipane.

MINI CHERRY GALETTES DES ROIS

❋ Makes 12 • Prep 45' • Oven 15-20' • Easy ❋

For the filling:

1 small jar of pitted cherries
50g butter, room temperature
60g sugar
50g ground almonds
a pinch of salt
1 tsp cornstarch
1 egg
1 tsp Kirsch
cherry jam
1 almond

2x 230g all-butter puff pastry
1 egg yolk
1 tbsp milk

Preheat the oven to 180°C fan.

Drain the cherries, halve and set aside.

In a bowl, mix the butter and sugar until creamy. Add the almonds, salt, cornstarch, egg and Kirsch and mix into a frangipane batter.

Make the galettes in batches. Unroll one puff pastry disc and cut out as many 9 cm discs as you can. You want to get 12 discs in total, so knead together the remaining dough scraps, roll out and cut out more if necessary.

Place 6 pastry discs onto a baking tray lined with baking paper.

Put a bit of cherry jam into the middle of these discs, leaving an uncovered edge of about 2 cm around the jam. Top the cherry jam with 1 teaspoon of the frangipane mix, then put 4 cherry halves on top. Tuck an almond into the centre of one of the cherry stacks – this will be the hidden 'bean'.

Mix the egg yolk with the milk. Brush the bare edges of the frangipane-topped pastries with the egg wash. Place the remaining pastry discs on top of the frangipane mounts and press down the sides to seal the egg-washed edges.

Cut a shallow criss-cross pattern across the top of each pastry, making sure not to cut all the way through the pastry. Brush each pastry with egg wash.

Bake the pastries in the preheated oven for 15 to 20 minutes, then leave to cool on a wire rack. While the pastries are baking, prepare the remaining 6 galettes.

Serve the galettes warm or eat them soon after baking.

TIPS

• This recipe will leave you with some leftover cherries and frangipane. You can make a dessert with the filling: put the frangipane into a little ceramic mold, add the remaining cherries or other fruit and bake for 20 mins at 180°C fan.
• You can keep the cherry juice and drink it. I like mixing it with sparkling water to make a cherry *Schorle*.

No Luxembourg Christmas dinner is complete without a *bûche de Noël* – a festive Yule log covered in buttercream and embellished with seasonal decorations. My *bûche de Noël* is stuffed with festive mulled wine pears and covered with a white chocolate frosting. I have also swapped the traditional meringue mushroom decorations for mini meringue Christmas trees to make it look like a winter wonderland.

SNOW WHITE'S BÛCHE DE NOËL

❄ Serves 8 • Prep 3h • Fridge 2h • Worth the effort ❄

For the Christmas tree meringues:
See page 267

For the mulled wine pears:
300ml red wine
80g sugar
1 cinnamon stick
3 cloves
1 star anise
3 peppercorns
2 pears

For the whipped cream filling:
250ml cream
1 vanilla pod
1 sachet vanilla sugar
1 sachet *Sahnesteif*
  (a stabilizer for
  whipped cream)
2 tsp Kirsch

For the white chocolate frosting:
100g white chocolate
100ml cream
100g mascarpone

Start by making the Christmas tree meringues, they can already be made a day ahead (see recipe page 267).

For the mulled wine pears:
Put the red wine, sugar and spices into a saucepan over a medium heat and leave to simmer for 10 minutes for the flavours to infuse.

Peel and core the pears and cut into 1 cm cubes.

After 10 minutes, remove the aromatics from the wine, add the pears and simmer for 5 minutes. Take off the heat and leave the pears to infuse for another 30 minutes.

Drain the pears and leave to cool completely, discarding (or drinking) the mulled wine. Once cool, put into a bowl, cover with cling film and refrigerate for 1 hour.

For the whipped cream filling:
Put the cream into a bowl. Slice the vanilla pod lengthwise, scrape out the seeds and add them to the cream with the vanilla sugar.

Whip the cream until it starts to thicken. Add the Sahnesteif and Kirsch and whisk until stiff. Refrigerate until needed.

For the white chocolate frosting:
Break up the white chocolate and put into a saucepan. Add 50ml of cream and melt over a low heat, stirring until smooth.

Put into a bowl and leave to cool for 5 minutes. Add the mascarpone and beat until smooth.

Whip the remaining 50ml of cream until stiff and fold into the mascarpone mixture. Set aside at room temperature.

For the sponge base:
4 eggs
a pinch of salt
125g sugar
1 sachet vanilla sugar
125g flour
1 tsp speculoos spice
    mix
¼ tsp cinnamon

For the sponge base:
Preheat the oven to 180°C fan.

Separate the eggs and beat the egg whites with a pinch of salt until stiff. Put the egg yolks into a bowl and mix with the sugar and vanilla sugar. Add the flour and the spices and mix again.

Add the stiff egg whites to the bowl and fold in gently with a spatula until you get an even, aerated batter.

Distribute the batter on a baking tray lined with baking paper and form a rectangular shape of approximately 30x25cm.

Bake in the preheated oven for 10 minutes.

Lay out a damp cloth. As soon as the sponge comes out of the oven, turn it onto the cloth and peel off the baking paper. Roll the sponge up in the damp cloth and leave to cool on a wire rack for 20 minutes – this will prevent the sponge from breaking when you roll it later.

Assemble the bûche:
Unroll the cooled sponge base and spread the whipped cream filling all over the sponge, leaving a 5cm border on the top length.

Distribute the mulled wine pears along the middle of the whipped cream, so that you form a line of pears approximately 5cm wide.

Starting at the top, roll the sponge over the pears and towards you.

Cut off the sides of the log, so that you get two neat ends.

Lift the bûche onto a serving plate and fully cover with white chocolate frosting. Decorate with Christmas tree meringues and sprinkles and refrigerate for at least 1 hour before serving.

This bûche will keep in the fridge for 3 days.

TIP

You can make the mulled wine pears and the Christmas tree meringues a day ahead.

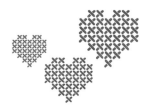

CHRISTMAS TREE MERINGUES

1 egg white
45g sugar
green food colouring
sprinkles, for
  decorating

Preheat the oven to 100°C fan.

Beat the egg white to soft peaks, gradually adding the sugar and beat until shiny and completely smooth.

Add some green food colouring and mix until evenly distributed. Put the meringue mix into a piping bag fitted with a star-shaped nozzle.

Pipe little Christmas trees the size of a 5 cent coin onto a baking tray lined with baking paper and decorate with sprinkles.

Bake the meringues in the preheated oven for 1½ hours. Leave to cool on a wire rack.

TIPS

• Keep the meringues in a dry place, as they are very sensitive to moisture and become really soft and sticky. They will keep in an airtight container for at least a week.

• You won't need all the meringues for the bûche. I like to fill the remaining Christmas tree meringues into little gift bags and hand them out as presents.

In December all the bakeries in Luxembourg sell these cute little men- and more recently women-shaped brioches. I've given my *Boxemännercher* a festive touch by adding warming spices and dried fruit – the perfect breakfast treat around Christmas time!

SPICED BOXEMÄNNERCHER

❄ Makes 8 • Prep 30' • Resting 1h • Oven 15' • Easy ❄

550g flour
1 cardamom pod
  (optional)
½ tsp cinnamon
a pinch of nutmeg
42g fresh yeast
250ml milk, lukewarm
100g sugar
25g candied orange
  peel
75g cranberries
a pinch of salt
100g butter, melted
1 egg + 1 egg yolk

For the 'starter', put the flour into a large mixing bowl. Crush the cardamom pod in a pestle and mortar, discard the shell and grind the seeds into a fine powder. Add to the flour together with the cinnamon and nutmeg, mix and make a well in the centre.

Crumble the yeast into a jar and mix with the lukewarm milk and 1 teaspoon of sugar until diluted. Carefully pour the yeasty milk into the well so it doesn't spill too far out of the well. Stir the yeast and the milk with a bit of flour from the sides of the well, so that you get a loose dough. Dust the starter with a bit of flour from the sides of the well. Cover the bowl with a damp tea towel and leave to rise at room temperature for 15 minutes.

Meanwhile, chop the orange peel and the cranberries.

After 15 minutes, add the remaining sugar, salt, melted butter, the whole egg, orange peel and cranberries to the 'starter' and mix with the kneading attachment of an electric hand or stand mixer. Work into a smooth dough, using your hands if necessary. Cover the bowl with the tea towel and leave to rise at room temperature for 30 minutes so the dough doubles in size.

Turn the dough out onto a floured surface and knock it back by briefly kneading it. Divide into 8 portions and shape each into an oval. Form a head at the top, then make a lenthgwise slit at the bottom and pull apart the two sides to form the legs. Make a diagonal slit on each side to form the arms.

Put the Boxemännercher onto two baking trays lined with baking paper, leaving enough space between them, as they will rise in the oven. Cover each tray with a damp tea towel and leave to rise for 15 minutes at room temperature.

Preheat the oven to 200°C fan.

After 15 minutes, beat the egg yolk and delicately brush the tops of the brioche buns with the beaten egg glaze. For the white eyes, mouth and buttons: mix a tablespoon of flour with a bit of water to form a paste. Dip a skewer into the flour paste and draw little eyes, a smiling mouth and buttons onto each Boxemännchen.

Bake the buns in the preheated oven for 15 minutes.

Stollen is my all-time favourite Christmas-time treat! I find it slightly disconcerting that *Stollen* logs start appearing on supermarket shelves as early as September these days – I prefer to wait until December, when I enjoy a slice of *Stollen* for breakfast every morning. A proper, yeasted *Stollen* takes quite a bit of time to make, as you need to let the dough rest and rise between kneading. But baking *Stollen* can be way faster than that! My super quick quark *Stollen* only takes half an hour to put together, followed by a brief stint in the oven! Yes, you need to soak the raisins overnight - but I'd say rum-soaked raisins are worth the wait!

QUICK QUARK STOLLEN

❖ Makes 1 Stollen • Prep 30' • Overnight soaking • Oven 1h • Easy ❖

250g raisins
100ml dark rum
2 eggs
130g sugar
1 sachet vanilla sugar
1 vanilla pod
280g butter
250g quark (less than 10% fat)
500g flour
5 tsp baking powder
3 tsp Christmas stollen spice
150g candied orange peel
50g crystalized ginger
40g icing sugar

Start by soaking the raisins a day ahead: put the raisins into a bowl, add the rum, stir and cover. Leave to soak for 8 hours or overnight.

The next day, put the eggs into a large mixing bowl and add the sugar and vanilla sugar. Slice the vanilla pod lengthwise, scrape out the seeds and add them to the eggs. Whisk until pale.

Add 200g of butter and whisk until creamy. Add the quark and whisk again until creamy.

Preheat the oven to 160°C fan.

In a separate bowl, mix the flour, baking powder and Christmas stollen spice. Gradually add to the wet mix and knead until the dough comes together.

Roughly chop the candied orange peel and the ginger and add to the dough with the soaked raisins and remaining liquid. Knead into the dough so the fruit is well distributed.

Place the dough on a baking tray lined with baking paper and mould into a log (it will be quite big, so if you prefer you can make two smaller logs instead). If you want to get the typical Stollen shape, you can mould the dough with your hands: run your hand along the centre of the log and slightly press down one side of the log so it's a bit less high than the other and there's a small indentation running along the middle.

Bake in the oven for about 1 hour – check whether the stollen is done by inserting a wooden skewer. If it comes out clean, the cake is done.

Melt the remaining 80g of butter. Take the Stollen out of the oven and brush with half the melted butter, then dust with half the icing sugar. Leave to cool for 15 minutes and repeat the process with the remaining butter and icing sugar. Leave to cool completely.

The Stollen keeps covered in foil in a cool place for a couple of weeks.

TIPS

• You can add marzipan to your *Stollen* – simply form a long marzipan log and place it along the centre of the *Stollen*, then fold over the edges to cover the marzipan.
• You can use any dried fruit you fancy in your *Stollen* – why not use dates, cranberries or apricots instead?

MY ESSENTIAL LUXEMBOURG INGREDIENTS

Mettwurscht

Mettwurscht is a smoked sausage made from pork and sometimes also beef. It is firm in texture, quite salty and very smoky in flavour. You're bound to find *Mettwurscht* at any Luxembourg barbecue and it tastes best with a generous squeeze of Luxembourg mustard. If you can't get hold of *Mettwurscht* for my recipes you can use firm cooking chorizo instead.

Träipen

Träip is a black pudding from Luxembourg – a blood sausage made from pork offal, vegetables and fresh blood. What makes it so distinct is its aromatic spicing, which means it's the perfect winter comfort food. *Träipen* are traditionally served with a side of braised red cabbage, apple compote, mustard and mashed potatoes.

Wäinzoossiss

A traditional Luxembourg pork and beef sausage made with wine. It's usually pan-fried and served with a creamy mustard sauce.

Judd

Smoked pork collar, which is traditionally served with potato puree and broad beans in a creamy summer savoury sauce. In Luxembourg, shops sell cooked and uncooked *Judd*. If you can't get *Judd* where you are, you can buy boneless smoked gammon instead.

Kachkéis

Kachkéis is a bit of a Luxembourg food oddity: a cooked cheese that is quite runny – think of the texture of glue: stringy and gloopy, but in a good, fondue-like way. It's usually spread on sliced bread and topped with Luxembourg mustard.

Traditionally, people would buy an uncooked, sausage-shaped *Kachkéis* curd portion and cook the *Kachkéis* themselves at home by melting and mixing it with milk or cream (you can find the recipe on my blog). These days you find ready-to-eat *Kachkéis* in every shop though. Varieties include low-fat and with herbs – the latter is my favourite.

Summer Savoury

Known as *Bounekräitchen*, this herb is one of the key ingredients in Luxembourg cuisine. It might be hard to find summer savoury where you are, so you could replace it with an equal mix of dried oregano and thyme – I find that comes closest to the real thing.

Beer

Luxembourg has a long-standing beer-brewing tradition, but these days there are only a few breweries left in the country. The most commonly brewed beer in Luxembourg is lager, but in my recipes I like to use *Wëllen Ourdaller* – an unfiltered dark beer made from malted barley and buckwheat.

Wine

Luxembourg is a proud wine-producing country and you can visit many wineries in the Moselle region, which borders Germany. The regional climate is favourable to white grape varieties. The most commonly grown varieties are Rivaner, Riesling, Elbling, Auxerrois, Gewürztraminer, Pinot Gris and Pinot Blanc. Luxembourg also produces excellent Crémant, which can, in my opinion, easily rival proper Champagne!

Honey Schnapps

Most Luxembourg distilleries make *Hunnegdrëpp*, a sweet schnapps made with Luxembourg honey. I always enjoy a *Hunnegdrëpp* at the annual fun fair, the *Schueberfouer*, which takes over the capital in late summer. Honey schnapps is not only a delicious tipple but also works as a fantastic ingredient in desserts.

Spelt

Spelt is an ancient grain that's mostly grown in the North of Luxembourg, in the Upper Sûre Nature Reserve. Most supermarkets in Luxembourg sell spelt flour, spelt flakes (an alternative to oats) and spelt pasta.

Mustard

Luxembourg mustard is very mild with a distinct aromatic taste. You can get hold of smooth and wholegrain varieties.

PICTURE INDEX

SNACKS & APPETIZERS

Mettwurscht Muffins
16

Gromperekichelcher Bites
19

Duo of Puff Pastry Swirls
20

Walnut Raisin Crackers
23

Beet Pickled Quails' Eggs
24

Smoked Trout Crêpe Rolls
27

Mini Bacalhau Bouchées
28

Courgette Roses
31

Raclette Quesadillas
32

SOUPS

Coconut Pumpkin Soup with
Coriander Pesto 40

Thai Bouneschlupp
43

Indian-style Lënsenzopp
44

Cream of Chicory Soup
49

Nettle Soup from
'De Grénge Schapp' 50

Onion Soup with Beer &
Bacon Dumplings 54

Wild Garlic Soup
57

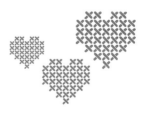

SALADS

Green Potato Salad with
Sausages 66

Chicory Salad with Walnuts
& Blue Cheese 69

Japanese Carrot Salad
70

Spanish Pasta Salad
73

Beetroot & Avocado Salad
74

Thai-style Cucumber Salad
77

Red Winter Slaw
78

SMALL PLATES & TARTS

Feierstengszalot Wraps
84

Steamed Mushroom Buns
88

Asparagus Toasts with
Goat's Cheese 91

Duo of Gaufres
92

Avocado & Egg Schmier
94

Strawberry Ketchup
95

Sweetcorn Tacos
98

Courgette Omelette with
Mint & Feta 101

Okonomiyaki Pancake
102

Gromperekichelcher
Cordon Bleu 110

Cauliflower Flammkuchen
113

Carrot Quiche with Goat's
Cheese 114

Träipen Quiche
117

Chicory Tarte Tatin
118

Kachkéis Fondue with
Mustard Croutons 121

Kachkéis Aligot
122

Asparagus with Béchamel
125

Gebootschte Potatoes with
a Fried Egg 126

PASTA

Judd mat Gaardebounen
Cannelloni 132

Pastachutta
135

Creamy Broccoli Kniddelen
136

Smoky Brussels Sprouts
Spätzle 139

Lentil Spelt Pasta
140

MEAT

Curry Rieslingspaschtéit
146

Traditional Rieslingspaschtéit
147

Beef with Egg Sauce
153

Wäinzoossiss Toad in the
Hole 154

Choucroute
158

Cider Chicken with Hasselback
Potatoes 160

Lemongrass Côtelettes
164

Côte à l'Os with Horseradish
Butter 166

Chilli con Mettwurscht
170

LuxemBurger
174

Pulled Pork with Bacon-
Wrapped Pears 178

Venison Stew with Kniddelen
& Pomegranate 180

FISH & SEAFOOD

Almond Butter Trout
186

Salmon en Croute
189

Sole & Salmon Roulades
190

Thai-style Mussels
193

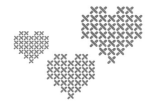

DRINKS

Strawberry G&T
200

Kir Popsicles
203

Quetschen Kippchen
204

Rhubarb Vodka
207

Rhubarb Mess
214

Spiced Orange Cream
217

Nutty Tiramisu
218

Patriotic Vacherin
220

Poire Belle Hélène My Way
224

Baked Apples
227

Red Wine Damsons with
Financiers 228

Raspberry & Blueberry
'Mille-Feuille' 231

Honey Schnapps Truffles
232

Redcurrant Jelly
235

CAKES & PASTRIES

Luxembourg Cookies
242

Fortune Cookie Wäffelcher
245

Buttery Jam Schuedi
246

My Marble Cake
249

Rhubarb Tartelettes
250

Buttery Pear Cake
253

Apple Pastéis de Nata
254

Bamkuch
256

Verwuerelter
260

Mini Cherry Galettes
des Rois 262

Snow White's Bûche
de Noël 264

Spiced Boxemännercher
269

Quick Quark Stollen
270

INDEX

Almonds
Almond Butter Trout 186
Buttery Pear Cake 253
Cauliflower Flammkuchen 113
Creamy Broccoli Kniddelen 136
Honey Schnapps Truffles 232
Mini Cherry Galettes des Rois 262
Red Wine Damsons with Financiers 228
Red Winter Slaw 78

Apple
Apple Pastéis de Nata 254
Baked Apples 227
Chicory Salad with Walnuts & Blue Cheese 69
Choucroute 158
Cider Chicken with Hasselback Potatoes 160
Smoked Trout Crêpe Rolls 27
Träipen Quiche 117

Asparagus
Asparagus Toasts with Goat's Cheese 91
Asparagus with Béchamel 125

Avocado
Avocado & Egg Schmier 94
Beetroot & Avocado Salad 74

Bacalhau
Mini Bacalhau Bouchées 28

Bacon
Asparagus Toasts with Goat's Cheese 91

Cauliflower Flammkuchen 113
Choucroute 158
Côte à l'Os with Horseradish Butter 166
Cream of Chicory Soup 49
Gebootschte Potatoes with a Fried Egg 126
Gromperekichelcher Bites 19
Onion Soup with Beer & Bacon Dumplings 54
Pulled Pork with Bacon-Wrapped Pears 178
Venison Stew with Kniddelen & Pomegranate 180

Beans
Chilli con Mettwurscht 170
Côte à l'Os with Horseradish Butter 166
Judd mat Gaardebounen Cannelloni 132
Thai Bouneschlupp 43

Beef
Beef with Egg Sauce 153
Côte à l'Os with Horseradish Butter 166
Feierstengszalot Wraps 84

Beer
Chilli con Mettwurscht 170
Onion Soup with Beer & Bacon Dumplings 54
Wäinzoossiss Toad in the Hole 154

Beetroot
Beet Pickled Quails' Eggs 24
Beetroot & Avocado Salad 74

Biscuits/Cookies
Apple Pastéis de Nata 254

Fortune Cookie Wäffelcher	245
Luxembourg Cookies	242
Verwuerelter	260

Bounekräitchen/Summer Savoury

Judd mat Gaardebounen Cannelloni	132
Lentil Spelt Pasta	140
Nettle Soup from 'De Grénge Schapp'	50

Broccoli

Creamy Broccoli Kniddelen	136

Cabbage

Cider Chicken with Hasselback Potatoes	160
Okonomiyaki Pancake	102
Red Winter Slaw	78
Smoky Brussels Sprouts Spätzle	139
Träipen Quiche	117

Cakes/Tarts

Bamkuch	256
Buttery Jam Schuedi	246
Buttery Pear Cake	253
Mini Cherry Galettes des Rois	262
My Marble Cake	249
Quick Quark Stollen	270
Rhubarb Tartelettes	250
Snow White's Bûche de Noël	264
Spiced Boxemännercher	269

Candied Orange Peel

Quick Quark Stollen	270
Spiced Boxemännercher	269

Carrots

Carrot Quiche with Goat's Cheese	114
Indian-style Lënsenzopp	44
Japanese Carrot Salad	70
Pastachutta	135
Venison Stew with Kniddelen & Pomegranate	180

Cauliflower

Cauliflower Flammkuchen	113

Cherries

Mini Cherry Galettes des Rois	262

Chicken

Cider Chicken with Hasselback Potatoes	160

Chicory

Chicory Salad with Walnuts & Blue Cheese	69
Chicory Tarte Tatin	118
Cream of Chicory Soup	49

Chocolate/Cocoa

Honey Schnapps Truffles	232
My Marble Cake	249
Poire Belle Hélène My Way	224
Snow White's Bûche de Noël	264
Venison Stew with Kniddelen & Pomegranate	180

Cider

Cider Chicken with Hasselback Potatoes	160
Pulled Pork with Bacon-Wrapped Pears	178

Cinnamon

Baked Apples	227
Buttery Pear Cake	253
Cider Chicken with Hasselback Potatoes	160
Coconut Pumpkin Soup with Coriander Pesto	40
Duo of Gaufres	92
Honey Schnapps Truffles	232
Pulled Pork with Bacon-Wrapped Pears	178
Rhubarb Mess	214
Rhubarb Tartelettes	250
Snow White's Bûche de Noël	264
Spiced Boxemännercher	269
Spiced Orange Cream	217

Coconut Milk

Coconut Pumpkin Soup with Coriander Pesto	40
Thai-style Mussels	193

Coriander

Coconut Pumpkin Soup with Coriander Pesto	40
Curry Rieslingspaschtéit	146
Red Winter Slaw	78
Thai Bouneschlupp	43
Thai-style Cucumber Salad	77

Courgette

Almond Butter Trout	186

Courgette Omelette with Mint & Feta	101
Courgette Roses	31
Wild Garlic Soup	57

Cucumbers
Thai-style Cucumber Salad	77

Damson
Quetschen Kippchen	204
Red Wine Damsons with Financiers	228

Drinks
Kir Popsicles	203
Quetschen Kippchen	204
Rhubarb Vodka	207
Strawberry G&T	200

Feta
Chicory Tarte Tatin	118
Courgette Omelette with Mint & Feta	101
Sweetcorn Tacos	98

Fish/Seafood
Almond Butter Trout	186
Mini Bacalhau Bouchées	28
Salmon en Croute	189
Smoked Trout Crêpe Rolls	27
Sole & Salmon Roulades	190
Thai-style Mussels	193

Goat's Cheese
Asparagus Toasts with Goat's Cheese	91
Carrot Quiche with Goat's Cheese	114
Duo of Puff Pastry Swirls	20
Wild Garlic Soup	57

Honey Schnapps
Honey Schnapps Truffles	232
Luxembourg Cookies	242

Judd
Choucroute	158
Judd mat Gaardebounen Cannelloni	132
Kachkéis Aligot	122

Kachkéis
Kachkéis Aligot	122

Kachkéis Fondue with Mustard Croutons	121
LuxemBurger	174

Kirsch
Kachkéis Fondue with Mustard Croutons	121
Mini Cherry Galettes des Rois	262
Redcurrant Jelly	235
Snow White's Bûche de Noël	264

Leek
Beef with Egg Sauce	153
Cider Chicken with Hasselback Potatoes	160
Feierstengszalot Wraps	84

Lemongrass
Lemongrass Côtelettes	164
Thai Bouneschlupp	43
Thai-style Mussels	193

Lentils
Indian-style Lënsenzopp	44
Lentil Spelt Pasta	140

Mango Chutney
Curry Rieslingspaschtéit	146
Red Winter Slaw	78

Mettwurscht
Chilli con Mettwurscht	170
Choucroute	158
LuxemBurger	174
Mettwurscht Muffins	16
Nettle Soup from 'De Grénge Schapp'	50

Mint
Coconut Pumpkin Soup with Coriander Pesto	40
Courgette Omelette with Mint & Feta	101
Red Winter Slaw	78
Strawberry G&T	200
Thai-style Cucumber Salad	77
Wild Garlic Soup	57

Mushrooms
Steamed Mushroom Buns	88

Mustard
Beef with Egg Sauce	153

Carrot Quiche with Goat's Cheese	114
Chicory Salad with Walnuts & Blue Cheese	69
Duo of Puff Pastry Swirls	20
Feierstengszalot Wraps	84
Green Potato Salad with Sausages	66
Kachkéis Fondue with Mustard Croutons	121
LuxemBurger	174
Okonomiyaki Pancake	102
Träipen Quiche	117
Wäinzoossiss Toad in the Hole	154

Orange

Spiced Orange Cream	217

Pasta

Creamy Broccoli Kniddelen	136
Judd mat Gaardebounen Cannelloni	132
Lentil Spelt Pasta	140
Pastachutta	135
Smoky Brussels Sprouts Spätzle	139
Spanish Pasta Salad	73

Pears

Buttery Pear Cake	253
Poire Belle Hélène My Way	224
Pulled Pork with Bacon-Wrapped Pears	178
Snow White's Bûche de Noël	264

Peas

Spanish Pasta Salad	73

Peppers

Chilli con Mettwurscht	170
Spanish Pasta Salad	73

Pomegranate

Red Winter Slaw	78
Venison Stew with Kniddelen & Pomegranate	180

Pork (including Judd)

Choucroute	158
Judd mat Gaardebounen Cannelloni	132
Kachkéis Aligot	122
Lemongrass Côtelettes	164
LuxemBurger	174
Pulled Pork with Bacon-Wrapped Pears	178
Thai Bouneschlupp	43

Potatoes

Asparagus with Béchamel	125
Cider Chicken with Hasselback Potatoes	160
Côte à l'Os with Horseradish Butter	166
Cream of Chicory Soup	49
Gebootschte Potatoes with a Fried Egg	126
Green Potato Salad with Sausages	66
Gromperekichelcher Bites	19
Gromperekichelcher Cordon Bleu	110
Indian-style Lënsenzopp	44
Kachkéis Aligot	122
Nettle Soup from 'De Grénge Schapp'	50
Okonomiyaki Pancake	102
Thai Bouneschlupp	43

Puff Pastry

Apple Pastéis de Nata	254
Chicory Tarte Tatin	118
Courgette Roses	31
Duo of Puff Pastry Swirls	20
Mini Bacalhau Bouchées	28
Mini Cherry Galettes des Rois	262
Salmon en Croute	189

Pumpkin/Squash

Coconut Pumpkin Soup with Coriander Pesto	40

Quinoa

Feierstengszalot Wraps	84

Raspberries

Raspberry & Blueberry 'Mille-Feuille'	231

Red wine

Pastachutta	135
Red Wine Damsons with Financiers	228
Snow White's Bûche de Noël	264
Venison Stew with Kniddelen & Pomegranate	180

Rhubarb

Rhubarb Mess	214
Rhubarb Tartelettes	250
Rhubarb Vodka	207

Rum

Baked Apples	227
Bamkuch	256

Quick Quark Stollen	270	Feierstengszalot Wraps	84
Verwuerelter	260	Pastachutta	135

Salad

		Träipen/Black Pudding	
Beetroot & Avocado Salad	74	Duo of Puff Pastry Swirls	20
Chicory Salad with Walnuts & Blue Cheese	69	Träipen Quiche	117
Feierstengszalot Wraps	84		
Green Potato Salad with Sausages	66	**Veal**	
Japanese Carrot Salad	70	Curry Rieslingspaschtéit	146
Red Winter Slaw	78		
Spanish Pasta Salad	73	**Walnuts**	
Thai-style Cucumber Salad	77	Chicory Salad with Walnuts & Blue Cheese	69
		Nutty Tiramisu	218
Salmon		Walnut Raisin Crackers	23
Salmon en Croute	189		
Sole & Salmon Roulades	190	**White Wine**	
		Choucroute	158
Sauerkraut		Creamy Broccoli Kniddelen	136
Choucroute	158	Curry Rieslingspaschtéit	146
LuxemBurger	174	Feierstengszalot Wraps	84
		Judd mat Gaardebounen Cannelloni	132
Soup		Kachkéis Fondue with Mustard Croutons	121
Coconut Pumpkin Soup with Coriander Pesto	40	Kir Popsicles	203
Cream of Chicory Soup	49	Mini Bacalhau Bouchées	28
Indian-style Lënsenzopp	44	Okonomiyaki Pancake	102
Nettle Soup from 'De Grénge Schapp'	50	Sole & Salmon Roulades	190
Onion Soup with Beer & Bacon Dumplings	54	Steamed Mushroom Buns	88
Thai Bouneschlupp	43	Traditional Rieslingspaschtéit	147
Wild Garlic Soup	57	Wäinzoossiss Toad in the Hole	154

		Yoghurt	
Spinach		Feierstengszalot Wraps	84
Salmon en Croute	189	Indian-style Lënsenzopp	44
Sole & Salmon Roulades	190	Rhubarb Mess	214

Strawberries

Strawberry G&T	200
Strawberry Ketchup	95
Patriotic Vacherin	220

Sweetcorn

Sweetcorn Tacos	98

Tomatoes

Chilli con Mettwurscht	170
Courgette Roses	31
Duo of Gaufres	92

Véronique lives and works in Luxembourg and specializes in wedding photography and portraits.

After graduating with distinction from the prestigious school of photography *Le 75* in Brussels, Veronique continued her studies in Fine Arts at the University of Strasbourg, where she accomplished a Masters degree in 2005.

Veronique was given a talent award by the *Centre National de l'Audiovisuel (CNA)* in 2001, followed by the publication of her monographic work *Reflections*. She has exhibited her works in Europe, the United States, India and China.

www.veroniquekolber.com
www.arthurandmary.com

Thanks to

Laura Letsch for being the best assistant ever and for making me laugh on a daily basis

Véronique Kolber for taking the beautiful pictures in this book and being a real sweetheart

Tim Lecomte + Fred Neuen of Radar for filming Anne's Kitchen Season 3 with me and 'surprisingly' liking all my dishes

Anika Raskopp for making me look pretty in the photos and in the TV show

My mum, Malou, for still taking out the red pen and testing the recipes in this book

Ben Péporté for sharing his secret for the perfect côte à l'os with me and for being my go-to person for all cheffy questions

Christine Faber for being the best sister in the world and going crazy about the okonomiyaki

Nadine Pyter for testing some of the recipes and really loving my Thai-influenced dishes

Carole Kremer for proof reading the English edition of this book

My dad, Marc, for invaluable business advice and support

Lena and Manuel Schortgen for going into book-round number 3 with me

Philippe Saliba + Eglantine Denis for designing the book layout with me

Steve Schmit for commissioning the accompanying 'Anne's Kitchen' TV Show on RTL Télé Letzebuerg

Eric Steichen for the nice behind the scenes photos of my studio

Eggo Kitchen for letting me design my dream studio kitchen and sponsoring my show

Marc Hoffmann and Cactus for sponsoring my show

Myriam Grof and KitchenAid for kitting me out with pastel kitchen equipment

Villeroy & Boch for providing me with the beautiful 'Vieux Luxembourg' crockery

More recipes
www.anneskitchen.co.uk

© 2016 Editions Schortgen
108, rue de l' Alzette
L- 4010 Esch-sur-Alzette
Luxembourg
editions@schortgen.lu
www.editions-schortgen.lu

Layout: Schortgen*grafic*
Print: Schortgen*bookprint*

1. Edition 2016
2. Edition 2017

ISBN: 978-99959-36-32-7

Anne's Kitchen ®
Recipes, Texts & Food Photos:
© Anne Faber
Photography: © Véronique Kolber
Book lining illustrations:
© Anne Faber

Villeroy & Boch - crockery and glasses:
Pages: 19, 91, 190, 201, 231, 245